D0913924

South Florida-Rochester-Saint Louis
Studies on Religion and the Social Order
EDITED BY

Jacob Neusner   William Scott Green   William M. Shea

ISLAM AND THE QUESTION OF MINORITIES

edited by
Tamara Sonn

ISLAM

——— AND ———

THE QUESTION OF

MINORITIES

edited by

Tamara Sonn

Scholars Press
Atlanta, Georgia

Islam and the Question of Minorities

edited by
Tamara Sonn

Published by Scholars Press
for the University of South Florida, University of Rochester,
and Saint Louis University

Library of Congress Cataloging in Publication Data
Islam and the question of minorities / [editor] Tamara Sonn.
      p.   cm. — (South Florida-Rochester-Saint Louis studies on
religion and the social order ; 14)
   Published…for the University of South Florida, University of Rochester, and Saint
Louis University"—T.p.verso.
   ISBN 0-7885-0309-X (alk. paper)
   1. Muslims—Non-Muslim countries. 2. Minorities—Islamic
countries. I. Sonn, Tamara, 1949–   . II. Series: South Florida-
Rochester-Saint Louis studies on religion and the social order ; v.
14.
BP52.5.I83   1996
297'.19783456—dc20   96-30752
                                         CIP

Printed in the United States of America
on acid-free paper

CONTENTS

INTRODUCTION

Tamara Sonn

Islam, to a greater extent than any other major religion, has been shaped by the questions Muslims have asked and by the willingness of Muslims to seek out their own religious authorities. The impetus for change in Islam has more often come from the bottom than from the top, from the edge than from the center.[1]

Bulliet's opinion regarding the development of Islamic ideologies, succinctly expressed above, has two important applications concerning Muslims and the question of minorities. First, it indicates the need for a shift away from the geographic paradigm in Islamic studies. While Muslim majority regions no doubt represent certain aspects of Islam in practice, there is no reason to assume that Muslims living as minority communities around the world are any less representative of Islamic society than those in the Middle East, for example. They simply represent different aspects of Islam in practice from those represented by their coreligionists who enjoy majority status. Indeed, the challenges they face by virtue of their minority status -- the questions they ask -- have implications regarding attitudes toward the state and pluralism which may well impact Muslim majority communities, as well.   Furthermore, the interaction between majorities and minorities within a single country has demonstrably affected developing Islamic identities. The purpose of this book is to explore these implications.

The volume consists of a series of invited papers dealing with specific perspectives on minority issues as they affect Islamic society today.   Rather than an exhaustive survey of Muslim minorities around the world, this collection consists of studies of unique aspects of the question of minority status in contemporary Islamic society. The contributors were asked to discuss (1) representative examples of Muslim minority communities and the complexity of issues they face; (2) examples of the interplay between Muslim minority and majority communities; and (3) the significance of the question of minorities in Islamic societies, including examples of the interplay between Islamist groups with Muslim minorities within Muslim countries.

TRADITIONAL ISLAMIC VIEWS ON MINORITY STATUS

Islamic life is based, theoretically, on God's revealed plan, Shari`ah. The divine will for human behavior was interpreted by scholars from the earliest days of institutionalized Islam and ultimately set out in specific legal codes of *fiqh*, the science of Islamic law. The intellectual activity required to interpret the divine will for human implementation is known as *ijtihad*, creative thinking, or "intellectual jihad," as some scholars have put it.[2]   Although modification and updating of Islamic law has continued throughout the centuries, the accepted wisdom from the late eleventh-early twelfth century on was that the basic outlines and essential features of Shari`ah had been established for all time. In words that have become very controversial in the present century, "the gate of ijtihad" was closed.[3] The phrase has become very controversial because the identifying characteristic of contemporary Islam is the need for renewal and reform, and -- despite a vast range of opinions about the nature and extent of that reform -- it is virtually unanimously agreed that ijtihad is essential to the process.

Whether one agrees or not that Islamic tradition overall needs significant rethinking, there are some areas in which it is clearly necessary. Those are the areas not specifically dealt with in the classical codes. Islamic law was codified by and for Muslims living in a predominantly Muslim world. That world was identified, in fact, as *dar al-islam*, the "abode of Islam." (Although this teminology does not appear in the Qur'an, "dar al-Islam" became the most common designation for the Muslim community among the classical legal scholars.[4]) Dar al-Islam was distinguished from *dar al-`ahd*, the "abode of covenant," *dar al-sulh*, the "abode of truce," and *dar al-harb*, the "abode of war." It referred specifically to those territories in which the law of Islam prevailed, a situation that was possible only because the vast majority of the population was Muslim. Dar al-`ahd and dar al-sulh were both regions whose leaders had agreed to pay the Muslim leaders a certain tax and to protect the rights of any Muslims and/or their allies who dwelt there, but who otherwise maintained their autonomy, including their own legal systems; dar al-harb was a region whose leaders had made no such agreement and where, therefore, Muslims and their allies, unprotected by law, were technically under threat.

This classification, although now essentially defunct, has nevertheless not been superseded. Yet it raises significant questions about the identity of Muslim communities. It is predicated on the premodern reality of legal systems specific to religious communities. The modern reality, by contrast, is one of nation states with laws based on truths about all human beings assumed to be self-evident and on human rights assumed to be universal. Modern legal systems, at least theoretically, no longer pertain to individual religious groups alone but to all the citizens of a particular geographic location, regardless of religious affiliation. Those laws pertaining to specific religious groups alone (such as those concerning ritual and modes of worship, dress, ornamentation and hygiene, and dietary laws) are relegated to the private sphere and may not interfere with rights considered by the majority to be universal. In this context, the dar al-Islam classification, with its implication that being truly Muslim means living under Islamic law, is called into question.

This is particularly true for the increasing number of Muslims living in non-Muslim majority countries. Muslim majority countries account for only about three-quarters of the nearly one billion Muslims in the world today. What is more, Muslim communities in Canada and the United States, for example, or South Africa or France, are permament; they do not consider themselves temporary residents, guests of a hostile majority. Through participation in democratic political systems, they are increasingly integrated into pluralist societies. The Muslim population of the world today is, in other words, global. While some, no doubt, harbor the belief that one day the entire world will submit to Islamic law, the majority accept the reality of pluralism as part of the divine plan. As the Qur'an puts it, "If your Lord had so willed, He would have made mankind one community, but they continue to remain divided." (11:118)

This view was discussed at a recent conference of prominent Islamist scholars held at the University of London.[5] The conference was convened to honor Fathi Osman, a senior scholar of Islam and well-known proponent of pluralism. In *The Children of Adam: An Islamic Perspective on Pluralism,* for example, he argued:

> Since the world is coming closer together as a result of miraculous developments in the technology of transportation and communication, global diversity has become a fact that has to be accepted intellectually and morally, and secured and sanctioned legally, by all groups throughout the world....Pluralism, also, requires a serious approach towards understanding the other and constructive cooperation for the betterment of the whole. All human beings should enjoy equal rights and opportunities, and all should fulfill equal obligations as citizens of a nation and of the world. Each group should have the rights to organize and develop, to maintain its identity and interests, and each should enjoy equality of rights and obligations in the state and in the world.[6]

Osman supports his views, which were applauded at the conference, with Qur'anic references:

Divisions into peoples and other groups with common
origin are acknowledged in the Qur'an (49:13), and
nothing is wrong with it so long as such divisions do
not hinder universal human relations and
cooperation, and are not abused through chauvinistic
arrogance and aggression. The Qur'an indicates that
God and his teachings should be put above any
allegiance to a particular group or land, and so long as
this principle is observed, allegiance to one's family
and other human gatherings and to one's homeland is
recognized (9:24).[7]

Osman devotes an entire chapter, "The Children of Adam," to
demonstrating that diversity is part of God's plan and must be
recognized as such in Muslim institutions. Therefore, he concludes:

Muslims, like adherents of other religions of the
world, have to live with non-Muslims within a given
country. Muslim citizens of a country can have their
ethnic or doctrinal differences within themselves or
with other Muslims in the world. Muslim unity does
not require that Muslims form a single state -- even
the caliphate always comprised different beliefs and
ethnicities.[8]

This new global Islam is the focus of a great deal of ijtihad
currently underway in the Muslim world. Islam has always
embraced pluralism within Islamic majority societies; it is well
known that religious freedom was institutionalized in the Islamic
world from the time of Prophet Muhammad. It was he who said
about Jewish tribes included in the Muslim community he established
in Medina in 622 c.e., "The Jews...are a community along with the
believers. To the Jews their religion and to the Muslims theirs."[9]
They were then guaranteed religious freedom and this became the
model of Islamic attitudes toward other religious minorities living in
their midst. But what are the rules for Muslim minorities living
permanently in non-Muslim majority states? If it is no longer the

case that to be truly Muslim means to live under Islamic law, then what does it mean? How are Muslims to interact with non-Muslims? Furthermore, what about Muslim minorities within Muslim majority countries? Since Islamic law is based on an assumed homogeneous Islam, it does not recognize minority groups within the Muslim community. But the modern world has brought to light the reality of Muslim ethnic minorities within Muslim countries. The articles collected in this volume deal with these issues. Recognizing that these are just some of the questions about minorities raised by changed realities in the modern world, we hope this volume will be followed by others offering further discussions on the question of minorities in Islamic society.

IDENTIFYING THE ISSUES

The volume begins with an historical piece offering a framework for recognizing the significance of questions "from the edge," to use Bulliet's phrase. In "Abduh and the Transvaal Fatwa: The Neglected Question," John Voll reexamines Abduh's famous fatwa (authoritative legal opinion) in light of minority, rather than majority issues. As Voll points out, the fatwa is well known among scholars of Islamic modernism. However, discussions of it "generally ignore the fact that the request for the ruling came from a real geographic location, the Transvaal in South Africa." Indeed, because the fatwa has been dealt with only in the context of modern Islamic intellectual history, the section of it that pertains specifically to the South African experience is generally ignored. Voll reviews the fatwa, therefore, focusing on the significance of the fact that the request for it came from a minority community -- in this case, in South Africa -- emphasizing overall the need for understanding the specific situations in which minorities live. Finally, he speculates on possible reasons for the generally truncated treatment of the fatwa thus far, as well as what such questions may reveal about the interaction between "the edge" and "the center," that is, between minority issues and majority viewpoints.

Voll begins by summarizing the questions that prompted the fatwa. The first concerned the permissibility of wearing European-style hats. The second was whether or not Muslims are allowed to eat meat slaughtered by Christians ("without saying the Bismallah"). These two questions were not unique to either minority experiences in general or the southern African experience in particular. Many Muslim men had begun to adopt European-style dress, including hats, particularly in urban centers where they carried on business with Europeans. And many were coming into contact regularly with Christians as a result of spreading colonial rule; the permissibility of eating meat prepared by them was therefore also an increasingly common question. As Voll says, "These questions involve practical issues of daily life for Muslims living in pluralistic, modern societies and Abduh treated them in this way." Abduh's "most flexible and inclusive interpretation" of each question is usually taken by commentators as a reflection of his modernist ideology, in contradistinction to the traditionalists who criticized his responses. Characteristically placing greater emphasis on intention than the specific action in question, Abduh responded that so long as the wearing of the strange hats was simply a pragmatic matter, it was permissible. That is, provided it was not symbolic of rejecting Islam, there was no harm in donning a fedora. Abduh went into a bit more detail in his discussion of the second question, but concluded that there is nothing un-Islamic about eating meat slaughtered by Christians, provided "they consider it permitted by their faith." Indeed, it is clearly permitted to do so "as a way of preventing restriction on social relations with [Christians] and working with them."

The third question, however, the "neglected question," is one that does not pertain to pluralism in the ordinary sense of inter-faith questions. Instead, it concerns intra-Islamic pluralism -- that is, pluralism among schools of Islamic law. As is well known, there are four major schools of Sunni Islamic law: Maliki, Hanafi, Shafi`i, and Hanbali. While technically they are considered mutually acceptable, in reality they are quite localized; each school is dominant in specific regions. Therefore, al-Hajj Mustafa al-Transvaali, who formulated the question prompting the fatwa, wants to know if it is all right for Shafi`is to pray behind Hanafi imams, given the fact "that there is a dispute between the Shafi`is and the Hanafis regarding the obligation to say the Bismallah and regarding the saying of 'Allahu Akbar' on the two holidays." Voll points out that this is a very specific question indeed, not one that arises everyday even in the colonized Muslim world, and he stresses the importance of understanding those specific circumstances in order to grasp the significance of the question in the first place: "The question asked by al-Hajj Mustafa does...reflect an interesting and important dimension of the development of the Muslim communities in southern Africa. It is this dimension that...is worth pursuing as a way of going beyond the classical, Egypt-oriented descriptions of the Transvaal fatwa."

Voll then sketches briefly the history of Muslim communities in southern Africa. As we will see again in Jeppie's chapter on Muslim identities in South Africa, the vast majority of Muslims in the region are descendants of two distinct waves of immigrants. The first group, in the seventeenth century, were brought by the Dutch as slaves and political exiles from what is now the Indonesian archipelago, Malaysia, and East India to the nascent Dutch settlement in the region of the Cape of Good Hope. The second group came as merchants and indentured laborers in the nineteenth century, primarily from West India, and settled mainly in British-dominated Natal. The former were accustomed to Shafi`i law while the latter were traditionally Hanafi. So long as the two communities remained geographically isolated there was little concern over which school of law, with its attendant forms of prayer, dominated where. However, with the discovery of gold, the Transvaal became a major population draw and it was there that the two communities came face to face.

Abduh's response to the third question was, like his other opinions, flexible and inclusive. He expressed belief in the soundness of sincere prayer regardless of peculiarities of rite. More importantly, he stressed the unity of Islam, despite certain differences. He stopped just short of chastising anyone who demands uniformity of practice and concluded that "it is not rational," particularly for Muslim minorities, to be at cross purposes with one another on such issues. As Voll puts it, "Abduh's distinction that Islam is 'one din (religion)' rather than religions *(adyan)* is a strong critique which reminds the South Africans that partisanship for the law school creates a context that approaches unbelief."

In summary, Voll's article on Abduh's Transvaal fatwa focuses attention on three issues of concern in this volume. First, the problems faced by Muslim minority communities are real. They face challenges that are not directly addressed in classical law codes and that therefore raise novel questions requiring ijtihad or fresh thinking. This issue was apparent to Abduh as early as the turn of the present century and yet today, while the number of Muslims living as minorities has increased at an exponential rate, the lion's share of attention is still given to Muslim majority communities. Secondly, questions of minority status in Islam are not confined to inter-faith situations, but include intra-Islamic issues, as well. Finally, the questions raised by al-Hajj Mustafa arose in specific circumstances in the southern African milieu at the turn of the century and understanding them requires an awareness of what those specific circumstances were. But the answers elicited by Abduh were likewise specific to his circumstances. As Voll notes, Abduh's responses came to be a matter of serious debate within the Muslim majority community which was itself undergoing transition. And while Abduh was -- and in some cases continues to be -- severely criticized by traditionalist Muslims, his "flexible and inclusivist" orientation has undoubtedly entered the mainstream of Islamic thought. The questions raised at the geographical periphery of Islam, that is, have elicited responses that resonate throughout the Muslim world.

The remaining chapters similarly focus of questions specific to minority status, both inter-faith and intra-Islamic. Identifying the particular circumstances surrounding those questions, the authors present issues and themes that may well have counterparts within Musim majority communities. In any case, they call attention to the reality of global Islam, some of the questions that reality raises for the first time in Islamic history, and some of the responses which may well affect the broader Islamic world.

THE DIFFICULTIES OF MINORITY STATUS

In "Muslims in Germany: The Struggle for Integration," Abdul Hadi Hoffmann offers a firsthand account of the difficulties encountered by Muslim minority communities in a sometimes hostile environment. Although there have been small groups of Muslims living in Germany over the past several centuries, Hoffmann reports, the current Muslim population of over two million people has its roots in the groups of laborers brought, in accordance with government policy, to fill the needs of a booming economy in the 1960s. Workers were recruited from Turkey, Morocco, Tunisia, and Yugoslavia (as well as Italy, Greece, Spain, and Portugal) under the assumption that they were "guest workers" who would return to their homelands in due time. The government was quite unprepared for the eventuality that they would make Germany their home.

But that is just what happened. The 1973 oil embargo brought fears of economic recession and strains on the federal budget due to a return of unemployment. The German government therefore tried to reduce the number of foreign workers, but their efforts were unsuccessful. Indeed, the "guest laborers" began to exercise their rights under a number of international accords and bring their families to join them, thereby increasing their community. The number of political exiles from Muslim countries such as Syria, Iran, and Algeria also increased, further augmenting the Muslim population in Germany.

Hoffmann himself is among the estimated 100,000-200,000 ethnic Germans who have declared themselves Muslim in recent years. As a professional political official, his perspective on German prejudice against Muslims is unique.

Hoffmann's observation that there is a strong association between German national sentiment and Christianity is, of course, not surprising. What is revealing in Hoffmann's account is the perception that reaction against ethnic Germans who declare themselves Muslim is in many ways stronger than that against immigrant Muslims. Hoffmann reports that he spent sixteen years working for the political party of Helmut Kohl, the Christian Democratic Union (CDU). During the last five years of that time he served as press spokesman for the party in the city of Bonn and head of journalistic services for public relations and the campaign staff at the party's federal headquarters.   Yet very soon after his declaration of Islam, a series of anonymous letters to newspapers began to demand that he be removed from office and even expelled from the party because he was a Muslim and "deceitful."   After a 1992 television appearance in which he spoke of his commitment to Islam, he personally began to receive anonymous letters referring to him as a "stinking Muslim" and a "defector" who should be shot.

Ultimately, officials within the Christian Democratic Union succumbed to public pressure.   After Hoffmann's publication in 1995 of a book recounting his conversion experience, the party informed him that he would lose his job if he made any more unauthorized statements.   When two requests for authorization to give public lectures on Islam were denied, Hoffmann realized it was time to seek employment elsewhere.

It is widely known that Turkish Muslims have suffered violent attacks in recent years in Germany.   Hoffmann reminds readers that Muslims have been beaten and killed in several German cities, including Molln, Rostock, Hoyerswerda, and Solingen.   Yet Hoffmann believes the reaction against ethnic German Muslims is particularly fierce because the phenomenon flies in the face of the perception that true German nationality precludes affiliation with a non-Christian religion.   Therefore, anti-Islamic prejudice is demonstrated not only against Germans who become Muslim but also against non-Muslims who defend the rights of Muslims or even study Islam.   This was demonstrated recently when German scholar Annemarie Schimmel was honored for her distinguished contributions to the study of Islam.[10]   There was a public outcry against Schimmel for studying Islam sympathetically rather than condemning terrorism. Perhaps also at work in the negative reactions to ethnic German Muslims is the fact that ethnic German Muslims know their political rights and have the ability to exercise them.   Hoffmann believes this is very threatening to chauvinistic Germans.

Hoffmann then details the steps Muslims have indeed taken in Germany to organize and establish themselves as an integral part of

German society. It has not been easy, he reports, because contrary to the stereotype, all Muslims are not the same. The German Muslim community includes Turks, Moroccans, Bosnians, and Arabs, among others. Each group has distinctive habits and wide-ranging political as well as religious views. Furthermore, as with all recent immigrant communities, the ethnic groups tend to socialize and worship among themselves, so that today there are in Bonn alone different mosques for each ethnic group. Nevertheless, after some thirty years of immigrant Islamic presence in Germany, there is now a generation of German-born and German-speaking Muslims who have managed to develop a number of successful national organizations. The Council of Islam, for example, an outgrowth of the Muslim Student Union, works primarily in the academic arena. The Central Council of Muslims in Germany was modeled on the Central Council of Jews and its purpose is specifically to serve as an advocate for Muslims at the federal level. It has been so successful that its chairman was officially received by President Roman Herzog in 1995.

Interestingly, Hoffmann contrasts the experience of German Muslims with that of French Muslims. He acknowledges that there are Muslims in Germany who believe Muslims should not interact with non-Muslims, but he claims that the majority are committed to integration within the overall German polity. "The young third generation Muslims want to join and in fact are joining the existing political parties." He observes, furthermore, that their ability to operate within the political system is the most direct means to that end.

There is no doubt still intransigence on the part of traditional ethnic Germans for whom Christianity is part of being German. There remains in German culture, as in all Euro-Christian culture, a lingering anti-Islamic prejudice, passed on subtly in the school curriculum. This prejudice is exacerbated by the indiscretion of contemporary media voices who characterize terrorism as "Islamic" -- again, an international phenomenon. Finally, there is the cult of the Enlightenment, according to which all positive human developments are associated with Euro-Christian society and that society is by definition in conflict with Islamic society. (This is a topic that will be expanded in Michel Machado's chapter on Muslims in France.) Yet Hoffmann concludes that the continued commitment of German Muslims to integration through participation in the political process may well assist in the breakdown of such stereotypes and allow for recognition and appreciation of continued Muslim contributions to the development of European society.

THE SIGNIFICANCE OF SPECIFIC CIRCUMSTANCES

In "Muslims in France: Islamism Confronts Jacobinism," Michel Machado discusses the complex roots of clashes between recent Muslim immigrants from North Africa and the growing number of Christian French who are attracted to the xenophobic platform of the *Front National* of Jean Marie LePen. Machado details four sources of misundertanding. The least troublesome are simple cultural differences. While sharing meals, including wine, with neighbors is central to traditional French patterns of socializing, prohibitions against consuming wine and pork products prevent Muslims from participating in this time-honored ritual. This, observes Machado, strikes those who are ignorant of Muslim practices as downright unfriendly. Similarly, the Muslim tradition of fasting during the daylight hours one month each year and then breaking the fast late at night in a sometimes noisy feast becomes a point of extreme annoyance for the uninitiated.

More troublesome than these rather superficial cultural differences between traditional ethnic French and the immigrants are economic factors which make the lower classes turn on one another in competition for scarce jobs and resources. In an era of rising unemployment, French Christians with long-established "French" identity find themselves resentful of the recent immigrants with whom they share their lowly status. This resentment is exacerbated when the immigrants find financial success. Machado mentions the fact that the traditional grocery, a staple of French neighborhoods, is undergoing a transformation under pressure from competing institutions run by the immigrants with differing business practices.

As in any country, such cultural and economic differences would be sufficient to cause communal friction. But the colonial history of France makes these problems even more difficult, particularly since the majority of French Muslim immigration is from the former French colony Algeria. Machado outlines the development of French control in Algeria, beginning with its convenience as a nearby source of cheap agricultural products for an industrializing France, as well as a penal colony. Ultimately, Machado notes, Algeria became three *departments* of the French government, rendering it no longer a colony but a part of France itself. Accordingly, Algerians were expected to accept French citizenship and, along with it, French language, education, and laws. The fact that the Algerians were content with Algerian citizenship, the Arabic language, and Islamic education and laws and therefore rejected French control led, of course, to French insistence on their "civilizing mission" in Algeria. Some eighty years of French control in Algeria resulted in the bloody war for independence (1954-62), in which Algerian efforts were intepreted as atrocities by many French. As Machado notes, there remains a reserve of anti-Algerian feeling among those ethnic French who lost family members or property during the war for Algerian independence.

Machado believes the most deeply rooted source of conflict between ethnic French and Muslim immigrants, however, is a difference in socio-religious paradigms. He is careful not to characterize all Muslims as adhering to the same paradigm. Yet he identifies a dominant theme in contemporary Islam, generally known as "Islamism," in which Islamic identity requires public displays of religiosity. Machado points to the wearing of the veil and public prayer during traditional French work hours as examples. The insistence on public religiosity, Machado observes, strikes at the very heart of modern French identity. Because of the complicity of the church in maintaining the French monarchy, Machado maintains that the principle of laicism or secularism, which he construes as utterly opposed to public religiosity, has been a vital component of French national ideology, Jacobinism. Along with humanism and freedom, laicism is considered a virtue. To question it is, for many French, to question the very structure of French society. Indeed, Machado notes that the insistence on laicism is absolutist and reactionary, itself intolerant:

[Jacobinism] claims universal hegemony upon the conscience, as did ancient clericalism....The official separation of church and state in 1905 consecrated the victory of laicism; it became mandatory and rabidly anti-clerical. Yet even with its hatred of religion Jacobinism could not avoid becoming the new-fashioned recipient of the hallowed. It is part of the ancient sacral continuum, only with a new foundational myth, the *Revolution,* a sacred discourse, *la morale republicaine,* a sacred space, *l'ecole republicaine.* The republican school would, with success, convert millions to the cult of the *Republic.*

The conflict of Islamism with this sacred laicism was inevitable, in Machado's analysis. French laicism became the analytic paradigm for those French already feeling economically threatened by immigrants or harboring resentment based on the Algerian war for independence. In this context, the desire to wear a veil to school became not just a matter of personal preference but a rejection of the foundational myth of modern France, as did the request for time off from work for Friday afternoon prayer.

Machado's analysis demonstrates the significance of understanding the specific circumstances of Muslim minority populations. Mere platitudes about pluralism will not be sufficient to advance the immigrants' desire to integrate into French society, nor will assertions of secularism convince anyone that French society is open. The specific ideologies of both communities must be aired, and the root causes of communal friction must be addressed. Machado concludes by observing that accommodation will require mutual understanding and compromise at the local level -- in turn, establishing a model which may prove useful on the global level.

THE LURE OF IDENTITARIANISM

In "Commemorations and Identities: The 1994 Tercentenary of Islam in South Africa," Shamil Jeppie analyzes another little discussed challenge of minority status: confusion among religious and ethnic identities. He begins by summarizing what many believe is the history of Islam in South Africa. According to literature promulgated during the 1994 festivities celebrating three centuries of Islam in southern Africa, it all began with the arrival of one Shaykh Yusuf in the Dutch colony at the Cape of Good Hope in 1694. Shaykh Yusuf, a religious scholar from Macassar, was a political prisoner of the Dutch East India Company, exiled from his native land for his opposition to Dutch colonial activities there. Banished to a rural area northeast of the Cape, he is credited with establishing the first Muslim community in southern Africa. The end of the apartheid government and the holding the first all-race elections in South Africa also took place in 1994, making the time ripe for celebration and facilitating the association of contemporary themes of Islam as a perennial struggle for social justice with the nationwide rejoicing at the end of a patently unjust political system.

Jeppie's description of the South African Muslim communities reveals, however, that this is a bit of a simplification. In fact, as noted by Voll, the majority of the Muslim population of South Africa, less than 2% of the country's overall population, is divided between two distinct cultural groups. Those descended from the early community established by Shaykh Yusuf and other slaves brought by the Dutch from what are now Malaysia and the Indonesian archipelago as well as East India, especially Bengal, are generally known as the Cape "Malays". (The "Coloureds" were another classification according to the Population Registration Act of 1950, although many use the terms "Malay" and "Coloured" interchangeably.) The "Indians" or "Asians" are descendants of a 19th-century wave of immigration from West India. The former are concentrated in the Cape region, while the latter are concentrated in Transvaal and Natal. For the "Indians," South African Islam was established in Natal in 1895 by Soofie Saheb, and there is a signficant difference between the "Islam" of the community established by Shaykh Yusuf and that which developed among the Muslims of the later immigration. Yet despite such differences among Muslims in South Africa and their very varied histories, Jeppie observes that "[t]he organizers [of the tricentenary celebrations], as public historians, scripted a consensus Islamic narrative." As Jeppie notes, celebration of the tricentenary of Islam in South Africa was carried out virtually entirely in the Cape region and by the Cape "Malay" Muslims. Indeed, despite the fact that only half the Muslims in South Africa are in the Cape region, the celebrations were characterized by "local Malay ethnic themes; a revived Malay identity pervaded a fair number of the festival's activities and was unmistakeably part of the most signficiant events."

In addition to this imaginary homogenization of South African Muslims, Jeppie points out several historical factors which call into question other themes of the tricentennial, such as the fact that the Republic of South Africa was not even established until 1910, and that not all Muslims were opposed to slavery or even to Apartheid. Indeed, Shaykh Yusuf was a slaveholder. Nevertheless,

> [t]he tercentenary of Cape Islam and the end of more than "three hundred years of minority rule" was a tidy and valuable coincidence which was not lost on the organizers of the festivities. The parallel narratives of Muslim subordination since even before their arrival, indeed their very landing premised on colonial domination and resistance, on the one side, and on the other, the long dark night of white minority rule over the black populace made useful publicity for Muslims and the Tricentenary. It aligned them discursively and imaginatively with the authentic and victorious historical forces at the appropriate moment, even though it transgressed all historical complexity and factuality.

In Jeppie's analysis, it is certainly understandable that a minority population would find a focus of identity in aspects of their ethnic background -- religious, culinary, etc. However, he also points out that applying the "Malay" ethnic label to Cape Muslims despite the "highly heterogenous" nature of the population, had its origins in the domination of that very community by the European minority. Designating the entire community "Malay" was convenient for "ruling class racialistic arguments and the development of segregationist policies -- with their divide and rule rationale -- which became the fully-blown Apartheid from the late 1940s onwards." Jeppie asserts that this spurious identity was further promulgated by "its white folklorists and ethnographers, most notably I.D. duPlessis, who were devoted to preserving aspects of the supposedly vanishing Malay culture, customs, language, and so on." But the organizers of the celebration, Jeppie points out, apparently oblivious to the subtly racist nature nature of such characterizations, seemed to embrace the stereotype. For example, an arts and crafts exhibition associated with the tricentenary was held at the Castle of Good Hope, despite the fact that "the castle was constructed by the first Dutch colonists and became a symbol of white minority rule, and thus the venue itself was steeped in colonial symbolism...." Furthermore, the articles chosen and the layout of the exhibit were "a conservative affirmation of stereotyped ethnic identity in the sphere of material culture and practice."

The tricentennial did include contemporary themes from the South Africans' very real struggle against oppression. Organizers of the celebration orchestrated a mass rally in Cape Town, instructing participants to march from District Six, an area many non-Europeans were forced to evacuate under one of the most hated pieces of Apartheid legislation, the Group Areas Act, and therefore a symbol of protest against oppression. Muslims from throughout South Africa made significant contributions to that struggle. Yet even that authentically South African component was overlain with exotic cultural associations, including Middle Eastern. Participants were asked to dress in white, like Islamists portrayed in news stories of the Iranian revolution or pilgrims to the Islamic holy cities Saudi Arabia. At the same time, the organizers of the rally wore contemporary Malaysian clothing which, Jeppie notes, "no local has ever worn," in what appeared to be efforts "to lead the Muslims back to their imaginary Malay origins and educate them in their true Islamic heritage and Malay tradition." The latter theme, he reports, was reiterated in speeches by invited representatives of the Malaysian government. This, despite the fact that Shaykh Yusuf and the majority of early Muslim slaves and exiles to South Africa came from what are now parts of Indonesia, not Malaysia, and a significant portion of the Muslim population has a distinctly Indian heritage.

Exploring these and other anamolies involved in the tricentennial events, Jeppie suggests that the reason the "return" to even an imaginary ethnic identity was so attractive was due to residual effects of Apartheid. The separateness of the Muslim communities was imposed by the ethnic Europeans. The defeat of the Apartheid system was not sufficient to reverse the ideology of separateness. Indeed, the lifting of Apartheid left a kind of valence for national affiliation which the Malaysian government was happy to fill. As Jeppie puts it, "At least some leading members among the planners were thoroughly seduced by the attractive power of the contemporary Malaysian state and its promotion of Malay identity." Jeppie goes on to speculate about the reasons the Malaysian government was anxious to encourage such an identity. Among them he finds internal Malaysian economic competition between the Muslim community and its non-Muslim Chinese population. He points out that the idea of a "Malay dispora" has been useful to the current prime minister in efforts to support the notion of a Muslim economic revival. This was the context, Jeppie reports, in which the tricentennial organizers received "handsome monetary support" from the Muslim Malaysian business community.

Jeppie concludes that the tendency to confuse ethnic and religious identity, or the lure of what Francois Burgat calls "identitarian" religion, particularly in the context of a history of minority marginalization, is understandable but unfortunate. Not only does it further the cause of those who marginalize the minorities in the first place, but it trivializes and even obfuscates the real contributions of the communities to South African culture. It negates "local cultural innovation" and denies the fact that "cultures are not transported, but made." Indeed, South African "Islam" is an imaginary identity, as is "the South African community." There is no single identity, but a vast and dynamic range that includes contributions from various regions and ideologies. The effort to homogenize the society under any rubric, Jeppie feels, is inherently oppressive and must be resisted in favor of continued evolution, autonomy, and intellectual diversity:

> The inclusive, democratic, egalitarian, and non-racial discourse of the progressive Muslim organizations of the 1980s should not now be forgotten. If representatives of the newfound ethnicity, with its wealthy connections, contribute to the type of isolation, insularity and belligerent communalism rampant elsewhere in the world (including Africa), they ought to be scorned and rejected by "South Africa" and its Muslim population.

THE CHALLENGE OF INTRA-ISLAMIC MINORITIES

Jeppie's concerns about the divisiveness of ethnic distinctions within the context of a single religion resonate with those expressed by Haldun Gulalp in "Islamism and Kurdish Nationalism: Rival Adversaries of Kemalism in Turkey."[11] Dealing with intra-Islamic minorities, Gulalp analyzes the interplay between developing secularist and Islamist ideologies and Kurdish ethnicity in Turkey.

Although overlooked in the doling out of statehoods by the European victors of World War I, the Kurds are a distinct ethno-linguistic group whose native "Kurdistan" spans Turkey, Syria, Iraq, and Iran. Nearly half of the estimated 25 million Kurds today live in Turkey. Gulalp explains that their separateness has been exploited throughout the history of modern Turkey, beginning with the creation of the Republic of Turkey under Kemal Ataturk in 1923. Because of Ataturk's insistence on the geographic identity of the state, he denied the distinctness of Kurdish identity. They were Turks like the rest of the citizens or, more precisely, "mountain Turks," referring to the topography of their southeastern region. The basis of the previous, Ottoman ideology had been Islamic identity; Kemalism superseded that identity, rendering the Kurds' Islamic identity irrelevant. The new, nationalist ideology, however, resulted in enforcement of a new kind of homogeneity. Turks were expected to dress in a particular way; styles of dress associated with Islamic identity were ultimately banned. And Turks were expected to speak

Turkish.   As Gulalp observes, "Although formally a territorial concept, in reality Turkishness became a linguistic category." Because use of the Kurdish language called into question the new Turkish identity, and with it the very legitimacy of the new state, use of the Kurdish language was also banned.

The first organized Kurdish activity against the Kemalist state was a rebellion led by the leader of the Naqshbandi Sufi order, Shaykh Said, in 1925. Not surprisingly, the Shaykh used religion as the basis of his criticism of the secularist Turkish regime, which responded with further legislation against vestiges of religious communal identity and insistent assertions of "Western" rather than "Islamic" orientation.   As Gulalp points out, the Shaykh Said rebellion set the stage for "the Kemalist regime's perception of an intimate connection between the Kurdish and Islamic threats to its own stability."

Assimilation of Kurds into the dominant Turkish identity was possible, Gulalp points out, and certainly occurred, particularly in urban centers.   But assertion of Kurdish identity never ceased. Continued marginalization of the Kurdish community and denial of Kurdish identity by the Kemalist regime inevitably produced resentment of a kind ripe for political exploitation. According to Gulalp's account, this is just what has happened to the Kurds' desire for communal recognition.   Gulalp mentions that the first group seeking to expand its political base by championing Kurdish rights were the Leftists during the 1960s and 1970s. However, he devotes his attention in the chapter to the efforts of the more current Islamist movement of the 1980s and 1990s. This is a period of widespread "disenchantment with the nation-state and the rise of alternative projects of community formation -- Kurdism as an intra-national ethnic identity movement and Islamism as a supra-national civilizational movement." Like the Leftists before them, the Islamists have enhanced their viability by supporting the Kurdish cause.

The Kemalist government itself has even tried to parlay support for Kurdish rights, when convenient, into political gain. Such was the case during the Gulf War when, in a scarcely disguised effort to capture the oil-rich Kurdish province of Mosul from Iraq in return for supporting the U.S.-led coalition against Iraq, Turkish

President Turgut Ozal suddenly reversed Kemalist policy toward Kurds. He recognized Kurdish identity and legalized the use of the Kurdish language, at least for "non-political" purposes. As it happened, Ozal's expansionist dreams went unfulfilled. But his recognition of Kurdish nationalism continues to reverberate.

Besides his designs on Mosul, Ozal had another motive in supporting the alliance against Saddam Hussein. Following the collapse of the Soviet Union and with it, NATO's stated reason for existing, the threat of "Islamic fundamentalism" was used to shore up the Euro-American military alliance. Given the fact that the Turkish government continues to place its economic hopes on eventual inclusion in the European Union, Gulalp reports that it has attempted to position itself as a bastion against the "Islamic threat" in its post-Cold War dealings with the West. Unfortunately for it, however, its return to opposition to Kurdish nationalism following the Gulf War has foiled those efforts.

Indeed, having for the first time in the country's history allowed Kurdish identity into public discourse, the Kurdish cause was taken up by the leading Islamist party, Refah (Salvation). Calling for unity among all ethnic groups based on Islam, Gulalp reports, "Refah proposes official recognition of a distinct Kurdish ethnic identity and freedom of linguistic and cultural expression." This position is seen as simply a matter of consistency with the party's other planks: social justice and pluralism. Furthermore, Refah has been outspoken in its criticism of the U.S.-led embargo on Iraq. Since the embargo's devastating effects have been felt in the Kurdish regions just as they have impacted the rest of Iraq, this position has also enhanced Refah's standing with Turkey's Kurds.

Gulalp does not claim that Refah's support for the Kurdish cause is the sole reason for its recent victories, but he does point out that the policy certainly broadened the party's appeal. Although Gulalp's article was completed before the recent inclusion of Refah in Turkey's ruling coalition, the author notes that Refah's strategy was already effective, as evidenced in its success in local elections in March 1994. Of those in the Kurdish regions who voted (Gulalp notes that perhaps as many as half continued the policy of boycotting Turkish elections), the majority voted for Refah. Indeed, Gulalp notes, part of Refah's appeal is that it has modeled itself as a minority, "convincingly bill[ing] itself as the party of the 'periphery' against the 'center.' Today, political opposition in Turkey to such widespread social ills as poverty, unemployment, corruption and the like is represented primarily by Refah which has successfully tapped into popular disillusionment with the unfulfilled and impossible promise of 'catching up with the West' by following in its footsteps."

Gulalp concludes with a prediction proven accurate by recent developments in Turkey: that Refah's support will continue to grow. He therefore cautions against treating Refah and the sentiments it represents as a minority. As he has shown, minority politics are eminently open to manipulation, just as the Kurdish minority issue has become the "hinge" for Turkish domestic politics. "The Iraqi-cum-Kurdish turmoil, partly created and left in suspension by Western powers, has proven to be a tremendous boost to the popularity of Refah which campaigns on a platform of defying the West. The continuation of the Kurdish crisis only serves to strengthen Refah."

ISLAM AND THE QUESTION OF MINORITIES

As indicated above, one reason the question of minorities in Islam has received relatively little scholarly attention is that for most of Islamic history, the question has affected only a few people. This is no longer the case and indications are that the the reality of Muslims living among majority non-Muslim populations will continue for the foreseeable future. Another reason, however, concerns the way scholars have envisioned Islamic studies. In a recent plenary address to a meeting of the American Council for the Study of Islamic Societies, John Voll discussed the evolving nature of Islamic studies. He observed, "[W]e are in the middle of a very important transition in the intellectual and scholarly exercise of understanding Islamic societies."[12] He traced the West's earliest introduction to the Islamic world to travellers' accounts, complete with their fascination with "the exotic." These were soon superseded by classical Orientalism, supported by highly academic textual studies but still approaching the Islamic world as "other." In the post-World War II era, Orientalism fell into disrepute, having been associated with imperialism. The accuracy or inaccuracy of that association is not the issue for Voll. He believes that the next period of academic interest in the Islamic world, "area studies," grew out of a changed perception of scholarly needs in the West. Area studies, supported by "grand bureaucracies and administrations of centers," were multi-disciplinary approaches to societies in specific geographic units of interest to the West. Those that involved Muslims included the Middle East, South Asia, and Central Asia. Orientalism and area studies differ categorically from travelogues in that they are produced by academics with varying degrees of scholarly discipline. Nevertheless, Voll sees a common thread among the three in that they all treat the Muslim world as "the other." The Islamic world in scholarly study has gone, he says, from being the "'exotic object' of the travel accounts to the 'exotic subject' of the Orientalists to the 'knowable object' of area studies." But in reality, that otherness is breaking down. The terms "global" and "local" are no longer opposites. As Voll noted, papers on Malcolm X and Muslims in Beijing are presented at meetings of the Middle East Studies Association, which is supposed to be the standard academic association for scholars of the Middle Eastern geographic area. "The other" is now among us in reality, and this development must be reflected in our scholarly paradigms. That is why Voll suggests that the academic study of Muslims is at another transition point:

> [J]ust as we needed not necessarily repudiate, condemn, and jettison Orientalism in favor of area studies, now I do not think we need to repudiate, jettison, and condemn area studies in order to go to something new. However, I do not think that area studies in our contemporary world provide all the kinds of information that people need in order to understand things like the history of Islamic societies.

Orientalism was an improvement over travelogues; rather than relying on anecdotal reports it provided careful analysis of texts. Area studies went beyond Orientalism, beyond the texts to multidisciplinary study of the vast array of manifestations of life in a given region. Voll ended his address with a challenge. Quoting Constantin Cavafy's "Waiting for the Barbarians,"[13] he noted that the study of Islamic societies can no longer be accomplished in isolation from non-Islamic societies. It must develop ways to reflect the "globalization" and "glocalization" of Islam. This volume is an effort to respond to that challenge. As noted above, it is guided by recognition that the specific circumstances of each community must be studied in their uniqueness. It is further informed by recognition that minority communities affect the larger communities in which they participate, both Islamic and otherwise. That is, Bulliet's contention that Muslim majority communities are influenced by developments in Muslim minority communities is extended; majority communities are likewise influenced by and through their interaction with minority communities, blurring the distinction between "us" and "them". Whether or not this approach to Islamic studies is an adequate response to Voll's challenge, it is hoped that this study of some aspects of minority issues in Islam will be followed by others to provide a fuller understanding of the contemporary realities of Islamic life.

---

[1]Richard Bulliet, *A View from the Edge* (New York: Columbia University Press, 1994):195.

[2]See Fazlur Rahman, *Islam and Modernity: Transformation of an Intellectual Tradition* (Chicago: University of Chicago Press, 1982):7.

[3]For a discussion of the continuing controversy surrounding the purported cessation of ijtihad, see Tamara Sonn, *Interpreting Islam: Bandali Jawzi's Islamic Intellectual History* (Oxford: Oxford University Press, 1996), Introduction.

[4]The usage is generally traced to hadith (extra-Qur'anic traditional) reports. See discussion by A. Abel, "Dar al-Islam" in *Encyclopedia of Islam* (Leiden: E.J. Brill, 1963) II:127.

[5]"A Conference in Honour of Dr. Fathi Osman," School of Oriental and African Studies, University of London, July 6-7, 1996, sponsored by the Islam and Modernity Forum, London.

[6]Mohamed Fathi Osman, *The Children of Adam: An Islamic Perspective on Pluralism* (Washington DC: Center for Muslim-Christian Understanding Occasional Paper Series, Georgetown University):1-2.

[7]Ibid., 3.

[8]Ibid, 2-3.

[9]For the entire text of the "Constitution of Medina," reportedly dictated by Muhammad, see W. Montgomery Watt, *Islamic Political Thought: The Basic Concepts* (Edinburgh: University Press, 1968):130-34.

[10]See, for example, her *Gabriel's Wing* (Leiden: E.J. Brill, 1963); *The Triumphal Sun* (London and The Hague: East-West Publications, 1978); *Islam in the Indian Subcontinent* (Leiden: E.J. Brill, 1981); *As Through a Veil* (New York: Columbia University Press, 1982); *Mystical Dimensions of Islam* (Chapel Hill: University of North Carolina Press, 1985); *And Muhammad Is His Messenger* (Chapel Hill: University of North Carolina Press, 1985).

[11]For treatment of another example of the interplay of developing Islamism with minority identities, see Ghada Hashem Talhami, *The Mobilization of Muslim Women in Egypt* (Gainesville: University Press of Florida, 1996).

[12]John O. Voll, "Globalization, Glocalization, and the Study of Islam," Plenary Address, 13th annual conference of the American Council for the Study of Islamic Societies, May 3, 1996, Villanova University.

[13]Voll cited Edmund Keeley, ed., *The Essential Cavafy.* Trans. Edmund Keeley and Philip Sherrard (Ecco Press, 1995). The pertinent lines:

> And now, what's going to happen to us without barbarians?
> They were, those people, a kind of solution.

Chapter 1

ABDUH AND THE TRANSVAAL FATWA: The Neglected Question

John Obert Voll

The Transvaal fatwa (authoritative legal opinion) issued by Muhammad Abduh in 1903 is one of the most famous documents of early Islamic modernist thought. It is at least mentioned in most discussions of Abduh's life and thought. However, these discussions generally ignore the fact that the request for the ruling came from a real geographic location, the Transvaal in South Africa. Instead, analyses of the fatwa deal with the issues generically as they relate to the life of Muslims in the modern world. Even the identity of the person who submitted the questions to Abduh is usually ignored in most discussions, so that the most thorough scholarly analysis of the fatwa, for example, simply notes that the questions had been submitted by "a Muslim of the Transvaal"[1] rather than giving the name of al-Hajj Mustafa al-Transvaali.

One result of this more general approach is that one particular question of the three submitted tends to be neglected or ignored, and this is the question that relates most specifically to the context of Transvaal. It is useful to try to place the Transvaal fatwa in its South African context as well as in the contexts of the politics of Cairo at the beginning of the twentieth century and of the life of Muslims trying to cope with the pluralism of the modern world. This can help us to see the broader contexts and the specific problems which are involved in the development of Islamic modernist thought as articulated by Muhammad Abduh.

THE FATWA

First, however, it is helpful to look at the fatwa itself in the more standard context of analysis. Muhammad Abduh, after a career as a political activist working with Jamal al-Din al-Afghani, a time in exile, and then a time as a legal scholar and official, was appointed the Grand Mufti of Egypt in 1899.[2] This appointment did not represent significant support for Abduh from local Muslim authorities, either in al-Azhar or in the palace of the Khedive. Instead, it reflected the view of the British occupation authorities who were prone to making comments like, "The Grand Mufti, Sheikh Mohamed Abdou, is an enlightened man, who does not stand very well, in consequence, with the retrograde sheikhs of the El-Azhar University."[3]

As Grand Mufti, Muhammad Abduh directly involved himself in the process of judicial review in a way that sometimes brought him into conflict with Egyptian administrative officialdom. It had become the custom for previous Grand Muftis simply to sign prepared forms rather than undertaking a review of cases submitted to the Mufti's office. Abduh, in contrast, insisted upon his being permitted a full review of case materials. Abduh also changed the existing practice by "giving fatwas in response to questions presented by individuals."[4] It was as an answer to questions submitted by an individual that Abduh issued the Transvaal fatwa.

As a result of these factors, Abduh was involved at times in political controversies as the Grand Mufti. Often the debates reflected the underlying issues of Egyptian politics rather than a clear division of views based on Islamic scholarship. In 1903-1904 the debate over the Transvaal fatwa reflected such a basic political dispute within Egypt. Rashid Rida, in his biography of Abduh, describes the attempts at refuting the fatwa as being a "cavalry charge of writers prepared by the Khedive" in an effort to intimidate the Mufti.[5]

The questions submitted by al-Hajj Mustafa did, in fact, raise important and controversial issues for Muslims living in the modern era. The three questions were:[6]

> 1)   There are individuals in the country of Transvaal who wear European-style hats in the performance of their business and in order to gain profits for themselves. Is that permitted?
>
> 2)   The manner in which [the Transvaal Christians] butcher animals differs [from Muslim procedures] because they hit cattle with an axe and after that, they slit the throat without saying the Bismallah, and they also butcher sheep without saying the Bismallah. Is that permitted?
>
> 3)   Shafi`is perform prayers standing behind Hanafis without saying the Bismallah, and they also pray behind them on the two holidays. It is well known that there is a dispute between the Shafi`is and the Hanafis regarding the obligation to say the Bismallah and regarding the saying of "Allahu Akbar" on the two holidays. Is it permitted to say prayers in this way, each behind the other?

These questions involve practical issues of daily life for Muslims living in pluralistic, modern societies and Abduh treated them in this way. He gave relatively extended discussions in answer to each of these questions, and, in each answer he opted for the most flexible and inclusive interpretation of the issues. With regard to the wearing of a European style hat, his answer was that if the reason for wearing such a hat was a pragmatic one, and not an expression of an intention to "leave Islam and enter a faith other than Islam,"[7] then the action was not to be considered repugnant. He presented a longer discussion of the issue of whether or not it was permissible to eat meat that had been butchered by Christians in a manner that did not conform exactly to Muslim rules for slaughter. He cited Surah 5:7 and then concluded: "Therefore, the verse is unambiguous in absolutely permitting [the Christians'] food, just so long as they consider it permitted by their faith, as a way of preventing restriction on social relations with them and working with them."[8]

It was the answer to the second question that caused the most controversy in Egypt. The political rather than the theological nature of the conflict was emphasized, as Rida noted, by the fact that although the Khedive and nationalists like Mustafa Kamil criticized the permission given by Abduh for Muslims to wear Western clothes and eat meat slaughtered and prepared by Christians, the Khedive and Kamil regularly themselves wore such clothes and ate such food.[9]

Conservative Muslim scholars outside of Egypt who were critical of such decisions also concentrated on the issues involved in the first two questions and seem to have ignored the third. One example is the refutation of modernism written in 1912 by Maulana A.A. Thanwi in India. Maulana Thanwi stated: "It is a common error nowadays that mutual transactions and politics are not supposed to be a part of religion and of the Shariah. Taking them to be merely social matters, people make them dependent upon personal opinion and the exigencies of the age, and believe themselves free to act as they like in these things....It is not permissible for a Muslim to simulate the infidels either in dress or in modes of food and drink."[10] Nowhere in his discussion of modernism does Thanwi refer to the position taken by Abduh with regard to the third question.

These two answers were the ones that also have been most noted by scholars dealing with the development of Islamic modernism. In most cases, the answer to the third question is simply ignored,[11] while others, like Malcolm Kerr, stated explicitly in such discussions that "we need concern ourselves only with the first two [questions]."[12] These authors all emphasize that Abduh was concentrating on the problems of life which would be faced by Muslims in a modern societal context dominated by non-Muslims. This fits into the general picture of Abduh presented by later scholars of a thinker and activist whose work is "characterized by a spirit of liberality and a freedom from bondage to tradition and a desire to render the religion of Islam entirely adaptable to the requirements of modern civilization."[13]

THE SIGNIFICANCE OF THE LOCAL CONTEXT

While the third question and Abduh's answer to it fits also into this general picture in a number of ways, this neglected question raises some aspects of Muslim life that are specifically related to the situation of Muslims in the Transvaal. It is, perhaps, because of this specificity that consideration of the question is neglected. The most thorough analysis of the Transvaal fatwa, that presented by Charles Adams in a chapter in *The MacDonald Presentation Volume,* illustrates the difficulties created by ignoring the South African context itself.

Adams states that "all three of these questions owed their origins to the fact that the Muslims of the Transvaal were a minority in the midst of a Christian majority."[14] This is clearly the case with the first two questions, but it is not apparent why the issue of Shafi`is praying behind Hanafis is the result of Muslims living as a minority among Christians. Adams makes it obvious that his analysis is not based on any knowledge of conditions in the Transvaal in his discussion of Abduh's answer to the third question. He begins by saying, "The third question...concerns the differences in the details of the prayer ritual as practiced by the four rites, or schools, of canon law which are recognized by orthodox Islam. Two only of the rites, the Shafi`ite and the Hanafite, are mentioned in the question, as the only ones, probably, involved in the situation in the Transvaal."[15] Adams then goes on to provide a description of these differences in prayer practices in general terms.

The question asked by al-Hajj Mustafa does, however, reflect an interesting and important dimension of the development of the Muslim communities in southern Africa. It is this dimension that, in the context of a discussion of Islam in South Africa, is worth pursuing as a way of going beyond the classical, Egypt-oriented descriptions of the Transvaal fatwa. This involves consideration of two specific aspects of the conditions leading up to the submission of the questions to Muhammad Abduh: these are the fact that it came from someone in Transvaal rather than some other part of South Africa, and the conditions existing in South Africa at the time of the fatwa.

For anyone who knows something about the history of Islam in South Africa, but who is not familiar with many specifics, the first question might be: why did this come from the Transvaal? There are two great centers of Muslim population in South Africa and neither of them is in the Transvaal. They are in the Cape Province area in the south and west and in Natal on the east coast. The Transvaal was an inland republic which was created by migrating Afrikaaners in the nineteenth century and was, until the 1880s, a rural, primarily agricultural republic dominated by whites of Dutch ancestry. The discovery of gold and the expansion of British imperial and commercial enterprises brought the Transvaal Republic more directly into the broader world. The Transvaal had few Muslims. Even after many years of broader regional integration and movements of peoples, the 1970 census records that only about 20% of the Muslims in South Africa as a whole lived in Transvaal. More than 30% of South African Muslims lived in Natal and virtually half of the Muslim population lived in the Cape.[16]

Muslims were and are a minority in every major area of South Africa. As a result, the first two questions answered by Abduh would relate equally to all South African Muslims. However, the Transvaal had a distinctive situation which made it somewhat different from the Cape and Natal in terms of the schools of Islamic law.

In the Cape, the overwhelming majority of the Muslims are identified in the historical record as "Coloured." These Cape Muslims came originally to the settlements in the Cape of Good Hope as a result of Dutch economic and imperial activity.[17] Some were brought from the islands of Southeast Asia as slaves by the Dutch as early as the seventeenth century and by the nineteenth century, the Cape Muslims were an established and growing part of the southern African population. Reflecting the Southeast Asian Muslim communities from which they came, the Cape Muslims were Sunni, following the Shafi`i school of Islamic law.

The other major Muslim community in South Africa had South Asian origins. In the second half of the nineteenth century the British brought into Natal a significant number of Indian contract laborers and some of these were Muslim. Later in the century, a new South Asian element arrived as Indian merchants and small business entrepreneurs came to southern Africa, with most going to Natal as well. The result was that by the end of the nineteenth century there was an established Muslim population in Natal whose origins were primarily South Asian. This community, reflecting its origins, basically followed the Hanafi law school.

When the Transvaal became a rapidly growing and prosperous economic area following the discovery and exploitation of the major gold resources, many entrepreneurs went to the region. These included a number of Indian Muslims who established themselves in the region as a small but important economic group. They were dispersed throughout the countryside as traders and shopkeepers and represented the majority of Muslims in the Transvaal.[18] By the second half of the twentieth century, more than 30% of the Indian Muslims in South Africa lived in the Transvaal, and they accounted for more than three-fourths of all Muslims in that province.[19] In effect, by the late nineteenth century, the Hanafi Indian Muslims were clearly the dominant group among the Muslims of the Transvaal.

There were, however, also Cape Muslims who had come to the Transvaal during the nineteenth century. Cape Muslims had developed relatively close ties to Afrikaans culture and their colloquial language became "predominantly Afrikaans" and there were reports that "Malays" had fought on the side of the Boers during the Anglo-Boer War at the end of the nineteenth century.[20] By the second half of the twentieth century, about 10% of the Cape Muslims of South Africa lived in Transvaal, where they were a little less than one-quarter of the Muslim population.

The two major South African Muslim traditions were thus mixed together in the context of the Transvaal at the beginning of the twentieth century. The law school of each community was an important part of the historic definition and identity of the groups. To be Cape Muslim meant, virtually by definition, to be Shafi`i, while to be an South African Indian Muslim meant adherence to the Hanafi school. These differences have been reflected in the training and education of the leadership, with Indian Muslims maintaining closer ties to the educational institutions of South Asia while the Cape Muslims were closer to the Arabic traditions, seeking training in Egypt and Arabia.[21] The contrast between Shafi'i and Hanafi was not then simply a matter of personal preference or legal practice; it involved the whole complex set of factors determining communal identity for minority groups in an ethnically and racially mixed social context.

One scholar has summarized the situation, even now, as follows: "The Cape or Shafi'i Muslims make use of Indian or Hanafi mosque facilities when they have no other choice and vice versa, but the two main groups largely keep to themselves and each prefers to make his own provisions. This is only natural since the two groups are part of a different geographic distribution, different linguistic, cultural and ethnic backgrounds."[22] The Transvaal is one of the few places where this clear separation was less possible. That is the place where, by the beginning of the twentieth century, both Cape and Indian Muslims were combined in the Muslim minority and needed to share resources to maintain Muslim communal life.

It is in the context of the Transvaal at the beginning of the twentieth century that the issue involved in the third question would arise: was it appropriate for a Shafi'i to pray behind a Hanafi prayer leader, even if the Shafi'i did not accept the Hanafi definition of what should be done during prayer? The smaller community of Cape Muslims in the Transvaal would find it necessary to use the prayer facilities of the larger Indian/Hanafi community, and guidance was sought as to whether or not this kind of integration was permitted.

The issue of conflict of interest between Shafi'is and Hanafis was not a new one for Cape Muslims, although the Transvaal context was new. In the Cape Province, some tensions between adherents to the two different law schools had already taken place. However, in this situation, although there were a few Indian Muslims in the Cape region, it was not a matter of tension between the two major Muslim ethnic groups. In Cape Town, the conflict revolved around the activities of a particular person, Abu Bakr Effendi.[23] Following a variety of disagreements within the Cape Muslim community, the British had requested that the Ottoman government provide the Cape Muslims with a religious guide. The result was the arrival in Cape Town in 1862 of Abu Bakr Effendi, a Kurdish scholar who had come to the attention of the Ottoman sultan. As an Ottoman scholar, Abu Bakr Effendi was a Hanafi and there were charges that the Sultan had sent him with instructions to convert the Cape Shafi`is.[24] A small group gathered around Abu Bakr Effendi and a young imam in a local mosque began to lead prayers according to the Hanafi interpretation. The attempt to remove the imam from his position resulted in a case which was decided by the Cape Supreme Court in favor of the young imam. However, most people then left the mosque and later a separate Hanafi mosque was established in a context of discrimination. It was only later that the Shafi`i-Hanafi tensions in the Cape were resolved.[25]

The Abu Bakr Effendi controversy involved a dispute about the actions of a particular individual and was not a conflict between two groups of people. The Hanafi involved was not part of the South African ethnic communal structure, but rather had come from the outside and was neither South Asian nor a "Malay." The Shafi`i-Hanafi dispute in the Cape was one that apparently all involved were willing to submit to the existing local judicial authorities. However, the situation in the Transvaal was different and, in that context, the question of Shafi`i-Hanafi relations was an issue of inter-communal relations and was submitted in traditional form to the Grand Mufti of Egypt.

THE IMPACT OF QUESTIONS FROM THE MARGINS

Muhammad Abduh's response to the question of Shafi`i-Hanafi relations raised important issues, both for the Muslims in South Africa and within the framework of Abduh's own concerns about the law schools. His response was:

> As for the prayer of the Shafi`i standing behind the Hanafi, I have no doubt regarding its soundness if the prayer of the Hanafi is correct according to his law school. The faith of Islam is one. It is necessary for the Shafi`i to know that his prayer leader is sound in the way he prays, without partisanship toward his prayer leader. Anyone who demands more than this regards Islam as a set of religions rather than one faith. It is

not warranted for the rational person to have a different purpose among Muslims who are few in number, in a place where all of its inhabitants are non-Muslim, except for those humble few. And God knows best.

It is not clear if Abduh was familiar with the details of the situation in southern Africa, but he did recognize that he was speaking to a group of people who were a very small minority in an overwhelmingly non-Muslim context. In speaking to these people, Abduh's message was clear and unambiguous: Muslim unity was the primary concern and arguing over the details of the differences between the schools of law was unacceptable. In the answer, Abduh's distinction that Islam is "one *din* (religion)" rather than being religions *(adyan)* is a strong critique which reminds the South Africans that partisanship for the law school creates a context that approaches unbelief.

This answer should not be neglected, as it seems to have been, for at least three reasons. First, and most simply, it is the answer which deals most specifically with the South African situation. There are not many places where the specific subject would be an issue for conflict. It makes, in other words, the Transvaal fatwa, a fatwa for the Muslims of Transvaal.

More broadly, however, Abduh's answer provides a very good statement of his views on adherence to the law schools in a context which is very concrete and explicit. Many scholars have noted that Abduh was opposed to *taqlid*, the relatively rigid adherence to prior precedents and opinions of the medieval scholars. It has also been recognized that Abduh worked for "a systematic comparison of all four [law schools], and even of the doctrines of independent jurists who advocated none of them, with a view to producing a 'synthesis' which would combine the good points of all....The logical implication of this method was the creation of a unified and modern system of Islamic law."[26] The "neglected" third answer provides an excellent indication of Abduh's thought on this matter, both in terms of the rejection of law school partisanship and in the affirmation that Islam is one.

A third reason why this answer deserves attention is that it provides a fuller appreciation of Abduh's conceptualization of the broader Islamic community. Scholars looking at the development of Islamic modernist thought frequently identify the pan-Islamic element as being associated with the ideas of Jamal al-Din and as essentially political. In this way, al-Afghani has been described as "a strenuous advocate of a unitary Islam who emphasized the concept of *ummah* (Islamic community) against the regionalism that in the next century was to break up allegiance to the Ottoman Empire into nationalism and the nation-state."[27] In general terms, al-Afghani is identified with activist pan-Islam and Abduh is usually described as having pulled back from that position to one of a more reformist program of societal reform.

The third answer in the Transvaal fatwa is, however, a strong reminder that while Abduh maintained a strong allegiance to the idea of a "unitary Islam," his pan-Islamic vision was conceptual and identity-oriented rather than regional and political. The statement in this third answer that "the faith of Islam is one" represents as unitary a view of Islam as that of al-Afghani, but it is more conceptually based. While the political pan-Islamists would bemoan the political disunity of the ummah, Abduh warns against the religious disunity. The third answer tells Muslims not to create different "religions" within the Islamic community. In the long run, this type of unitary or pan-Islam may be the more effective message for Muslims in the modern world.

The "neglected question" of the Transvaal fatwa is thus a very important one. It ties the fatwa to the specific situation of South Africa. At the same time, it is a strong reminder of the dimensions of Islamic modernism which aim at legal synthesis and reform and which also represents the intellectual -- and possibly more effective -- alternative to the political pan-Islam of the tradition of al-Afghani.

---

[1]Charles C. Adams, "Muhammad 'Abduh and the Transvaal Fatwa," *The MacDonald Presentation Volume* (Princeton: Princeton University Press, 1933; reprinted 1968):15.

[2]Two helpful short biographies of Abduh are Kenneth Cragg, "Abduh, Muhammad," *The Oxford Encyclopedia of the Modern Islamic World* (Oxford: Oxford University Press, 1995), 1:11-12, and Joseph Schacht, Muhammad Abduh," *The Encyclopaedia of Islam* (Leiden: E.J. Brill, 1991), 7:418-20.

[3]Rennel Rodd to Lord Lansdowne, Cairo, 9 August 1901. F078/5156. No. 93.

[4]Adams, "Muhammad Abduh," loc. cit., p. 14.

[5]Muhammad Rashid Rida, *Ta'rikh al-Ustadh al-Imam al-Shaykh Muhammad Abduh* (Cairo: al-Manar, 1350/1931), 1:667.

[6]The full text of the questions and Abduh's responses can be found in Muhammad `Amarah, ed., *al-A`mal al-Kamiliah li'al-Imam Muhammad `Abduh* (Beirut: al-Mu'assasah al-`Arabiyyah, 1974), 6:255-256. This is the text used as the basis for discussion in this paper, unless otherwise indicated. Different sources give slightly varying versions of the questions (see, especially Rida, *Ta'rikh,* loc. cit., 1:676). Adams ("Muhammad Abduh," loc. cit.) uses a text of the fatwa which appeared in a booklet specially published at the time, while `Amarah had access to and publishes the text as it appears in the Third Register of the registers of Dar al-Ifta', Number 190.

[7]`Amarah, op. cit., 6:255.

[8]Ibid., 6:256.

[9]Rida, *Ta'rikh,* loc. cit., 1:695.

[10]Maulana A.A. Thanwi, *Answer to Modernism,* trans. Muhammad Hasan Askari and Karrar Husain (Delhi: Adam Publishers, 1984):111 and 115.

[11]See, for example, the discussions of Abduh's fatwas in Osman Amin, *Muhammad Abduh,* trans Charles Wendell (Washington: American Council of Learned Societies, 1953):79, and Albert Hourani, *Arabic Thought in the Liberal Age, 1798-1939* (London: Oxford University Press, 1962):152-53.

[12]Malcolm H. Kerr, *Islamic Reform: The Political and Legal Theories of Muhammad Abduh and Rashid Rida* (Berkeley: University of California Press, 1966):145.

[13]Charles C. Adams, *Islam and Modernism in Egypt* (New York: Russell and Russell, 1933):80.

[14]Adams, "Muhammad Abduh," loc. cit., p. 18.

[15]Ibid., p. 21.

[16]These figures are taken from W.J. Argyle, "Muslims in South Africa: Origins, Development and Present Economic Conditions," *Journal of the Institute of Muslim Minority Affairs* 3/2 (Winter , 1981): 223.

[17]A useful summary of the history of Muslims in South Africa can be found in J.A.Naude, "Islam in South Africa: A General Survey," *Journal of the Institute of Muslim Minority Affairs* 6/1 (January, 1985): 21-33.

[18]Argyle, op. cit., pp. 246-48.

[19]See Naude, op. cit., p. 24, and Argyle, op. cit., p. 223.

[20]See Naude, op. cit., p. 25.

[21]Ibid.

[22]Ibid.

[23]This discussion of Abu Bakr Effendi is based primarily on Achmat Davids, "The Origins of the Hanafi-Shafi'i Dispute and the Impact of Abu Bakr Effendi (1835-1880)," *Pages from Cape Muslim History*, ed. Yusuf da Costa and Achmat Davids (Pietermaritzburg, South Africa: Shuter and Shooter, 1994):81-102.

[24]Ibid., 82.

[25]Ibid., 99-100.

[26]Hourani, op. cit., p. 152.

[27]Cragg, op. cit., 1:11.

Chapter 2

MUSLIMS IN GERMANY: The Struggle for Integration

Abdul Hadi Hoffmann

"We asked for workers, and we got human beings." Nobody today remembers who said this for the first time, but everybody agrees that it explains better than anything else the origin of Germany's Muslim minority, even though nobody thought about it at first. Industrialists and politicians were importing labor in the 1960s. Nobody at that time was prepared for the arrival of real people with real needs. No one thought much about the consequences of transplanting people from one culture to another. And not much attention was given to the fact that a large segment of the foreign "guest workers" population was Muslim.

NINETEEN SIXTY-ONE IN GERMANY

The economy was booming; about 500,000 job vacancies were registered, and only about 180,000 Germans were listed as unemployed. Importing foreign labor seemed to be the easiest way out of the labor shortage. At first only an initiative by German industry, the plan to import labor was soon sanctioned by the federal government by mutual agreement with foreign governments to recruit workers in their respective countries. Recruitment treaties were signed with Italy, Greece, Spain, Turkey, Morocco, Portugal, Tunisia, and Yugoslavia.

There was not much concern with the needs of and facts about these guest workers. Since they had come to work and were supposed to stay only for a short while, it seemed acceptable for them to live in dormitories and over-expensive rooms of apartments turned into hostels. "They are only here to save money for back home anyway," was the general opinion. Certainly no one was aware that this was the beginning of a Muslim community in Germany.[1] It was noticed that the guest workers from Turkey, Morocco, and Tunisia had different religious and dietary habits, but in the 1960s Islam was not an issue. It was the early Kennedy years: the Cuban Missile Crisis, the Berlin Wall. The only other international conflict worth arguing for or against was Viet Nam. The Middle East was a question of Israel versus the Arabs. At that time the problem was identified as "Palestinian terrorism;" the phrase "Islamic terrorism" had not entered our vocabulary. In Iran the Shah was ruling in splendor. The renaissance of Islamic movements was far in the future. As a consequence, the Muslim guest workers were left essentially to themselves.

THE END OF RECRUITMENT, THE BEGINNING OF "FAMILY JOINING"

By November 1973, however, the economic picture had changed. The federal German government began to fear the arrival of a recession due to increases in oil prices. They therefore decided to stop recruiting any foreign workers from outside the European Community. By that time over 900,000 Turks were living in Germany. The government hoped not only to stop the influx of non-European workers but also to stem the growth of the community already established. However, this attempt was not successful for two reasons: There was a change from the original policy of rotation whereby workers were only allowed short stays in Germany, and then sent home and replaced with a new crop of workers. Industry soon had found that it was not profitable to send back workers who had just been trained in the requisite skills. More importantly, workers found that a short time in Germany was not enough to earn the money needed to establish economic independence in their home countries. Therefore, they exercised rights they had been granted under a number of international agreements already in place, according to which the workers could bring their families to join them in their countries of employment. Thus, between 1973 and 1980 there was a constant influx of family members, increasing the Muslim foreign worker community population. In 1980 alone the number of new arrivals was 212,000.

In another effort to ease the pressure on the German labor market, the government of the Christian Democratic Union (CDU), which came to power in October 1982, passed a law to supply financial benefits for those workers who wanted to go back home. Some took the opportunity to leave. Furthermore, there was a slowdown in immigration; in 1983 and 1984 there were only about 42,000 new arrivals. Still, the total Turkish population in Germany stayed about 1.5 million. In recent years it has grown to over 1.9 million.

CURRENT POPULATION

Today in 1996 there are no precise figures reflecting the total size of the Muslim community. However, there is general agreement that the current Muslim population of Germany is around 2.2 million. In addition to the Turks, the largest portion of that population, this community is made up primarily of people from the Maghreb (North Africa) and Yugoslavia. A much smaller group are those Muslims who come officially to Germany to study. There are also those who come as refugees from their home countries: Muslims from Syria, for example, who fled the regime of Hafez al-Assad; and Muslims from Iran fleeing the political system there. Included among other Muslims from Algeria is a recent wave of refugees who supported the *Front Islamique du Salut* (FIS), also seeking political asylum in Germany.

Still another component of Germany's Muslim population are ethnic Germans who have accepted Islam as a matter of free choice. Here again figures are not very precise, and estimates range from 100,000 to 200,000, the truth being most probably in the middle somewhere. Many of them make this choice because they marry a Muslim. But there is also a small but constant flow of people who say the *shahada* (prayer asserting acceptance of the essential teachings of Islam) simply out of personal conviction.[2] To the traditional German population, which is deeply rooted in Christian tradition and does not readily take to "the exotic," this phenomenon is difficult to accept. This is especially the case if the people who "become Muslim" are visible in public life because of positions in government administration and/or politics. In such cases the reaction can be quite fierce.

Since the author of this chapter is one of those German Muslims not only whose life changed religiously but who has been subject to threats of all kinds and whose career took a decisive turn in a new direction, some details may be of interest here.

CHANGING DIRECTIONS

After sixteen years of active political engagement in the Christian Democratic Union including a variety of chairmanships at different levels, and in my fifth year as the head of the group of journalistic services for the public relations and campaign staff of the federal headquarters of Helmut Kohl's party, I said the shahada in 1989. It was a private religious decision based on three issues. First, I appreciated the fact that Islam does not know the concept of original sin, which had alienated me from the Protestant religion in which I was raised. Secondly, I fully accepted the absolutely monotheistic message of Islam, rejecting the concept of the Holy Trinity and Jesus as the son of God. In addition, I liked the fact that Islam does not have an institutionalized church. Except for my parents, my boss, my secretary, and a few "good friends" -- one too many, as it turned out -- I told no one of my decision.

Three days after my election to the office of press spokesperson for the CDU in the city of Bonn in 1990, anonymous letters told the daily papers of Bonn that the new spokesperson was a Muslim. They went on to claim that this fact had been kept from the members of the party deliberately, and that the new office should be taken from Hoffmann. Indeed, they demanded that he be expelled from the CDU. Fortunately, the journalists agreed not to publish these anonymous messages.

In 1992, in cooperation with the Jeddah-based International Islamic Relief Organization ("Igatha"), I organized the first of a number of trips for journalists to Zagreb and Split to inform them about what was going on in the former Yugoslavia. That summer I made my first public statement as a Muslim. This was followed soon by an appearance on one of the most widely watched national television talk shows, where I had twenty minues out of an hour to talk about the message of Islam and the changes it had brought to my life. Ever since that time I have been living with more anonymous letters calling me a "stinking Muslim" and a "stinking foreigner," showing the clear equation in the popular mentality of Islam and foreign-ness. I still get letters implying that I have somehow defected and informing me that defectors are being shot. People offer to come to my apartment and beat me up. Unfortunately, such threats are not extraordinary in Germany. Even non-Muslims receive them if they speak publicly in support of Muslims' rights. For example, priests and mayors who have come out in favor of building mosques in their towns also receive death threats. Again, the reaction is against what is considered exotic or foreign and therefore inimical to an assumed essentially Christian ethnic identity.

For a time the federal headquarters of the CDU defended my right to choose my religion and welcomed my public statements as proof of the liberal attitude of the party. But after a change in the administration of the party, my situation worsened. Thus, when the publication of my book *Zwischen allen Stuhlen: Ein Deutscher wird Muslim (Between the Stools: A German Becomes Muslim,* Bonn, 1995) was announced in the spring of 1995, I was told that if I made any more statements without authorization from the party, I would lose my job. When I duly sought permission to give two public lectures on Islam and was denied, I decided it was time to find another position. I then joined a public relations consulting firm in the private sector.

Of course, I am not the only German Muslim with problems like these. Murad Hofmann is the former German ambassador to Algeria and Morocco. During his tenure in the latter post he announced his second book about certain aspects of the Shari`a (the Islamic legal system) and was then fiercely attacked in the German media. A woman member of the federal parliament demanded that the foreign minister recall Hofmann from his post because Germany, in her opinion, should not be represented by "a medieval macho Muslim." Later, when it was pointed out that the book was not yet on the market when she had made the statement, she admitted that she had not even looked at the book. Her reaction, clearly, was not to the contents of the book but to the mere fact that a German was somehow associating with the despised foreigners.

A MATTER OF LIFE AND DEATH

The threats to German Muslims are, however, in no way comparable to the real violence committed against immigrant Muslims in Germany in recent years. On several occasions in different areas of Germany people have been beaten and killed because they have come here asking for asylum or because they were praying in a way that seemed strange to the ethnic German Christians. The cities of Mölln, Rostock, Hoyerswerda and Solingen -- where, in the most horrible incident of all, most of the members of a Turkish family were burned to death -- serve as reminders that the violent society which we thought belonged to the past is still a reality in Germany.

To a certain extent, of course, these fierce reactions can be explained. For one thing, some Germans feel those who reject their inherited religious tradition are traitors somehow. More importantly, the existence of Muslims of ethnic German origin also deprives the opponents of Islam of their basic argument: that Islam is foreign to Germany. It is easy to avoid dealing with the message of Islam when you are culturally distinct from its adherents. Differences in language and eating habits, it seems, act as a buffer between ethnic Germans and immigrant Muslims, allowing the former to maintain their conviction that Islam does not belong on German soil. But there are no such shields when these people confront Muslims who are ethnic Germans. Finally, German Muslims know their rights as citizens. They know the political framework and how to work within it to demand their rights. It is to be expected that they are much more determined to fight for their rights and enter the political field. Perhaps this appears to xenophobic Germans as a far more dangerous threat even than the "foreigners" for, in fact, joining the political fray is just what German Muslims have begun to do.

GETTING ORGANIZED

With the arrival of the families of the guest workers, it became apparent that Muslims were going to stay. Thus, they needed not only housing but access to schools for their children. They also demanded regulations to enable them to slaughter their animals in accordance with Islamic rules, they wanted to build prayer rooms, and they want to be able to bury their dead in a proper Islamic way.

But even with a Muslim population of 2.2 million, only one third of an overall population of 6 million foreigners living and working in Germany, it still remains easy for public opinion and politicians to ignore most of the needs of Muslims in Germany. This is because as foreigners they have not yet formed a voting constituency. Even if the Muslims are successful economically, as employees or self-employed, and even if their children leave university with excellent marks, they remain more isolated than other foreigners who come from Christian backgrounds, for example. The religious difference is sufficient to keep them "other."

Furthermore, despite the prejudices of Christian Germans, the Muslim community in Germany is not monolithic. It reflects the tremendous diversity in the Muslim world overall. If today, for example, you want to go to a mosque in Germany's former capital city of Bonn (poulation 300,000), you have a choice. You can go to the Moroccan *salle de priere,* to the Turkish mosque that used to be a carpenter's shop, to the former supermarket which is now the Afghani mosque, to another Moroccan mosque which was a car repair shop, or to the new Bosnian mosque, a former business office. Since the opening of the Saudi-financed King Fahd Academy, you can also go to the mosque proper which was built as a part of the academy.

Organization of such a diverse community is difficult since immigrants of the different nationalities tend to stick together. Not only in Bonn but throughout Germany they have their own communities and clubs based on the culture of the countries they come from -- even if this behavior is actually considered "un-Islamic." Cooperation among the various Muslim ethnic communities tends to be more evident in agreement on foreign policy issues than in intra-Muslim cooperation even within a single city. It was only three years ago, for example, that in the city of Mannheim all Islamic communities got organized and instituted an annual "Islam week" with very impressive lectures, open houses in mosques, and other cultural events. The majority of Muslims, however, still tend to socialize primarily among their ethnic communities. In other words, Muslims have made it very difficult for themselves to be accepted as partners in negotiations in the political life of Germany because their would-be German interlocutors simply can question whether any one group actually speaks with authority for the entire community, in order to shy away from dialogue.

Yet organization of the German Muslim community, essential for integration into German society overall, has proceeded apace. What then were the first steps toward gaining political integration and, closely related to it, religious acceptance for Muslims? The structure of political administration in Germany works on three levels: city councils, governments of the states *(Lander),* and the federal level. It was on the city level where the first steps toward organization and integration were taken. Muslims of the first generation, having gained their basic German language skills, managed to turn old supermarkets and factories into places for prayer. They also managed to arrange for those who could not be shipped back home for burial to be buried in an Islamic way in Germany.

Developing Islamic schools was more difficult, because education is in the political sphere of the states. Organization at this level requires far more organizational skill. It took almost thirty years and the growing up of what is called the "third generation" of Muslims, born in Germany and speaking German as their mother tongue, for organization of Muslims in Germany to be effective on this and the national level. By the early 1990s, the annual meeting of "German speaking Muslims," which brings together Muslims of all different nationalities living in Germany, had become the nucleus of state and national organization. Indeed, it is now so large that the organization holds two conferences annually in each of the major states, and one large national conference. At these conferences experiences are exhchanged, strategies are discussed, and, of course, cultural events are celebrated.

Such events have been effective in developing a national German Muslim consciousness and building networks among disparate communities. Phone calls, letters, and faxes have helped consolidate the German Muslims, as have personal visits. We have travelled from north to south, to show solidarity, to give advice, or just to sit and pray together. Thus, a new quality of togetherness has begun to develop among German Muslims.

The efforts to create a unified German movement have resulted in the creation of three organizations on the national level: *Islamrat fur die Bundesrepublik Deutschland und West-Berlin* (Council of Islam for the Federal Republic of Germany and West Berlin; "and West Berlin" was dropped after reunification), the *Islamisches Konzil* (Islamic Council), and the *Zentralrat der Muslime in Deutschland* (Central Council of Muslims in Germany). The Council of Islam, actually founded in 1986 in Berlin, has for a long time been a quiet advocate of dialogue. Having been founded ahead of its time, it had to wait and grow to play a significant public role. The Islamic Council is managed by the Muslim Student Union, and has strong contacts with foreign governments and donors. It works mainly in the academic field. In the spring of 1996, for example, it organized a small convention which instituted a working group for the establishment of a German chapter of the International Institute of Islamic Thought, founded in the United States twenty-five years ago.

The real breakthrough in public life was the establishment of the Central Council of Muslims in Germany, a name adapted from the Central Council of Jews. It was created in November of 1994 out of the former Committee for the Establishment of Islamic Slaughtering in Germany. The reason for its existence is directly linked to the structure of the German federal government. In order to be registered as an official lobbyist on the federal level, you have to be an incorporated association or society *(Verein)*. In order to get this registration -- that is, to play by the German rules -- the committee decided to become incorporated. It is truly a national organization. Its chairperson, Dr. Nadeem Elyas, is a physician from Saudi Arabia. The vice-chairpeople are German and Turkish, the secretary general is a Turkish Muslim, and the treasurer is a German Muslim. Furthermore, with statements about the rules for Islamic burials, which were distributed nationwide, and with the initiative for Islamic religious instruction in German schools in the German language, the committee has gained nationwide publicity and indications are that it is an accepted partner in dialogue today. In the summer of 1995, Dr. Elyas was the first "official" Muslim to be invited to a hearing in the federal parliament about organ transplantation. The most significant event on the way toward political recognition, however, was the invitation to the Central Council by President Roman Herzog to his residence in Berlin in December 1995. This was the first time a German president spoke officially to Muslims.

POSITIVE AND NEGATIVE INDICATIONS

These first, small steps towards influence differ greatly from what seems to be happening in France and England. In Germany there has been no tendency to form an Islamic party or parliament, as in Britain. The young third generation Muslims want to join and, in fact, are joining the existing political parties. There are, of course, many debates about whether it is Islamic to be involved in organizations with "unbelievers," but the majority of German Muslims seem to have made the decision to work and live with and inside German society.[3] And even with unemployment high, there is nowhere near the air of desolation and despair among German Muslims that we hear exists among Muslims in France. The trust in the German economy to speed up again and produce jobs is still there, as is the desire and ability to find a place within German society by working within the political process.

What is going to happen in the future is, of course, only a matter of speculation, and a positive and peaceful outcome is by no means guaranteed. I have mentioned the positive signs, but there are also some barriers against the integration of Islam into German society which must also be mentioned.

First, Germany, like other nations of the West, is supposed to be secularized and a country where the ideals of the Enlightenment are deeply rooted. However, if you look closely, this is not quite accurate. It is true that the churches have no official say in German politics. But the state does collect taxes from the Christians and distribute them to the churches. The churches are officially recognized as "corporations by public law," and as such their representatives sit on the boards of the broadcasting corporations as well as in the meetings of the (state) ministries of education, deciding religious curricula in schools where it seems only natural that Christian religious instruction is given. Indeed, the major political force in Germany, the party that has ruled the country since 1982, calls itself the Christian Democratic Union, implying that it derives its program from the roots of Christian ideology. Therefore, in spite of secular ideology, there is undeniably a public Christian presence in Germany. Nevertheless, in fairness it has to be noted that it was the churches that first encouraged a culture of dialogue with the Muslims. Both major denominations have appointed representatives whose only task it is to engage in dialogue with Muslim communities.

Secondly, the frame of mind of the German population has been shaped by history books which reflect 1400 years of Christian historical writing. While this is not always hostile to Islam, in many cases it is simply ignorant of Islam and, unfortunately, in some cases there is a distinct anti-Islamic bias.   Iranian-born Professor Abdoljavad Falaturi, from the Islamic Academy in Cologne (which moved to Hamburg in February of 1996), spent years analyzing Islam in German textbooks. Slowly the texts are being changed, partially due to honorable efforts like those of Sigrid Hunke in *Allah ist ganz anders: Enthullung von 1001 Vorurteilen uber die Araber (God Is Completely Other: The Dismantling of 1001 Prejudices about the Arabs;* Bad Konig, 1990). It is perhaps not surprising that Charles Martel, who stopped the Muslims at Tours and Poitiers in 732 c.e., is still described as a hero, as is Prince Eugen who defeated the Turks before Vienna in 1453. The spirit of the Crusades, however, is still evident and seems to stand in the way of appreciation of the contributions of Islam to world history, such as the fact that the cohabitation of the three Abrahamic faiths under Islamic rule in al-Andalus (Spain) produced an unprecedented high culture. Similarly, that Goethe's poetry would not be what it is without his knowledge of Arab-Islamic culture and religion, for example, or that Lessing wrote the play "Nathan der Weise" about the closeness of the three Abrahamic religions, and that Ruckert was motivated to attempt a German translation of the meaning of the Qur'an, seem to be quite overlooked in German higher education.

Finally, German Muslims face the same challenge that confronts Muslims everywhere: that all Muslims are made to be responsible by the media for everything any single Muslim does at any place in the world in the name of Islam. We all know that the *ummah* is the community of all Muslims and that it does not allow borders or nationalities to divide it. And we all know that it was the English and the French who divided their colonial possessions and thereby separated the Muslim world into different countries. Nevertheless, Muslims worldwide should not be held responsible for the actions of a few. Still, there is a strong tendency in Germany for the actions of some Muslims to be taken as representative of all Muslims' views. Thus, it becomes very difficult, particularly after the Gulf War, for example, to convince people that Islam is a message of peace.

This last phenomenon may be the most unexpected for citizens of the West who pronounce the shahada. We were brought up in the spirit of the Enlightenment and we exercised what we believed is our religious freedom. Yet suddenly we find ourselves in a situation where our former friends reject us, telling us we have turned our backs on Enlightenment principles. They believe we have joined a tradition that discriminates against women and rejects democratic values. These people, it seems, have turned Enlightenment principles, democracy, and human rights into a new kind of absolutist and intolerant religion. Many are not even willing to engage in dialogue. When they hear of the many structural analogies and shared values between Islam and Christianity, they dismiss it as propaganda. It is this intolerance that I find most disappointing. I feel that I have discovered an ironic twist in Enlightenment principles which I call the trap of Enlightenment.

Having exercised my religious freedom I expected to find tolerance but instead have found animosity and hostility, even from those who consider themselves the most enlightened.

To cut through these layers of public prejudice and misinformation is the first prerequisite to a wider acceptance of Islam in Germany. German Muslims -- of German ethnicity and otherwise -- are now cooperating in this endeavor. Those who grew up in Islam share their knowledge of the tradition with their sisters and brothers, and those who grew up in Western culture push the process of political integration. They understand both the political system which is key to integration and the prejudices that stand in their way.

However, working for acceptance in everyday life and in the political community is only one aspect of the struggle for integration. Of equal importance is the conflict for ideological hegemony being waged internationally. On the one hand is the school of those who, like German author Sigrid Hunke, speak of three heritages of Europe: the Judaic, the Christian, and the Arab-Islamic. On the other are those who, like Harvard University's Samuel Huntington, speak of the inevitable cultural clash betwen Islamic and Western civilization.[4] Huntington's theory, of course, has no foundation in European culture, as was demonstrated recently when he was invited by the prestigious Konrad Adenauer Foundation in Bonn. After his lecture he was confronted by a group of silver-haired former German diplomats who respectfully pointed out to him that he had no understanding of the cultural fabric of Europe, which incorporates "many beautiful and important threads of Islam." But I think European Muslims have an important role to play in this debate. We are in a unique position to be able to demonstrate that Europe -- and with it, Western civilization as a whole -- would scarcely be what it is without the Arab-Islamic heritage. From its role in the development and transmission to Europe of philosophy, mathematics, and science to the very institution of the university, the Islamic world is an integral part of what is now recognized as Western civilization. General acceptance of these facts will not only change the outlook of the Europeans toward their own culture, but will allow Muslims to feel that Western culture is not an alien and hostile phenomenon. This new attitude would characterize a Europe in which those who choose to may feel at home and with which those on the other side of the Mediterranean can communicate as cultural equals. The Mediterranean Sea would cease to be a border between an essentially Christian Europe and the non-Christian world, and become simply a sea connecting the North and the South. German Chancellor Helmut Kohl envisioned this possibility in his speech to greet Pope John Paul II in front of the Brandenburg Gate in the spring of 1996. He spoke for the union of all Christians: Catholics, Protestants, and the Orthodox. But he went on to encourage greater understanding of the shared heritage of the three Abrahamic faiths: the Jewish, Christian, and Muslim. If this sentiment takes root and grows, the Muslim minority in Germany might have a future after all.

---

[1]It must be mentioned that there have been small groups of Muslims living in Germany for the past several centuries. Prussian King Friedrich Wilhelm I was the first "importer" of Muslims, when in 1731 he incorporated twenty Turkish soldiers into his army.

[2]I do not use the terms "convert" or "become Muslim" generally because of the Muslim teaching that all people are born Muslim in nature *(fitrah)*; only the parents educate their children in different beliefs.

[3]If one uses the categories often used to describe variations within Islamic ideologies -- modernists, traditionalists, and tajdidists or "renewalists" -- one will find all three represented in Germany. The modernists tend toward secularism, and the traditionalists tend toward an isolationist stance. But the tajdidists are a solid majority in Germany.

[4]See Samuel Huntington, "The Clash of Civilizations?" in *Foreign Affairs,* 72/3 (Summer 1993):22-44.

Further Reading:

Abdullah, Muhammad Salim, *Was will der Islam in Deutschland?*
Bonn, 1995.

Hoffmann, Christian H., *Zwischen allen Stuhlen: Ein Deutscher
wird Muslim.* Bonn, 1995.

Hofmann, Murad, *Der Islam als Alternative,* 3rd edition. Munich,
1995.

-----, *Reise nach Mekka: Ein Deutscher lebt den Islam.* Munich,
1996.

Hunke, Sigrid, *Allah ist ganz anders: Enthullung von 1001
Vorurteilen uber die Araber.* Bad Konig, 1990.

-----, *Allahs Sonne uber dem Abendland.* Stuttgart, 1960.

Leggewie, Claus, *Alhambra: Der Islam im Westen.* Reinbek bei
Hamburg, 1993.

Ministerium fur Arbeit, Gesundheit und Soziales des Landes
Nordrhein-Westfalia, *Turkische Muslime in Nordrhein-
Westfalen.* Pulheim, 1995.

Sen Faruk and Goldberg, Andreas, *Turken in Deutschland: Leben
zwischen zwei Kulturen.* Munchen, 1994.

Chapter 3

MUSLIMS IN FRANCE: Jacobinism Confronts Islamism

Michel Machado

Examining the predicament of Muslims in France is critical
because of what it says about the larger picture of future relations
between Europe and the Arabomuslim world. After Algerian
independence (1962), Islamic migratory movements to France
generated a substantial minority of three to four million individuals
(7.3% of the French population). The presence of a vigorous
religious community in this highly secularized nation, however,
presents specific problems. France troubles some Muslims with its
irreligious, universal culture, yet astounds them with all the
amenities of modern life. French institutions and traditions reveal
recently immigrated Muslims as underdeveloped and seemingly
archaic. Would Muslims' integration into French society require
modification of some of the ideology underlying French institutions
as those in the French Muslim community who have voiced
ideological opposition to French secularism would have us believe?
These issues point to the seemingly insoluble conflict between a
secular nation and a predominantly religious community for the
anti-secularist Muslims have been successful in depicting Islam as an
oppositional force to assimilation into the French nation. Their
Islamist ideology compels the French nation to reexamine its

relationship with religion while Muslims in general struggle to acclimate to the French culture. How can Muslims integrate into French society fully and keep what is essential to their religion if it is, as claimed by some, antithetical to the existing French system? This dilemma is further complicated by the fact that traditional French values themselves are undergoing reevaluation inside the larger context of the European community.

I will begin my discussion of these issues by offering some definitions of key terms. I will then provide a brief history of the Muslim presence in France. And finally I will analyze the conflict about the veiling of schoolgirls and the demise of the Kelkal terrorist group, showing how these events relate on a symbolic level to the difficult dialogue between secularism and religion (here, Islamism) in France today.

DEFINITIONS

I use the term "France" to mean not only a nation but also an ideological construct centered on a strict Jacobin laicism. Laicism is an extreme separation of the church and state that tends toward antireligion. It has reigned supreme in French politics since the Third Republic (1871) and still is intolerant of other ideologies.

Similarly, there is a sense in which Islam is an ideological construct. We must distinguish between Islam as an essentialist ideology often represented as alien to the concept of state and nation as the French see them, and Islam as a generic term covering traditions claimed in vastly diverse ways by nearly all the representatives of the Maghrebi population living in France. The majority of Muslims practice their faith without ostentation and many are avowed secularists. In fact, Bruno Etienne claims that the majority reflect the French lack of enthusiasm towards religion. However, there is a vocal minority determined to impose its rather doctrinaire version of Islam on the majority. This version of Islam, anti-secularist and frequently traditionalist, is called Islamist. Islamists are the ones who use the term "Islam" as if it were univocal, and who tend to identify themselves publicly through styles of dress and mannerism.

The majority of Muslims in France are Sunni, yet not all are Arabs. Turks, Berbers, and Africans from Senegal cherish their ethnic peculiarities and form distinctive communities. Distrust among the various ethnic and cultural groups is significant. Arabs and Berbers, as well as Algerians and Moroccans, have strong differences. Turks tend not to interact with other Muslims. Soninges from Senegal disagree with Maghrebi Muslims about marriage with non-Muslims. Additionally, they practice female circumcision, unlike the majority of Muslims. Maraboutism, Sufism, and traditional witchcraft are evident in some Muslim communities, although they are condemned by the orthodoxy. Religious influences from Riyadh, Teheran, and Cairo also divide the believers, as do those of Algiers, Rabbat and Ankara. Also, there are some 600,000 Harkis in France, Muslims who were faithful to France during the Algerian uprising are therefore considered traitors by Algerian nationals. Yet despite these differences, those French who are prejudiced against Muslims often tend to treat all Muslims as despised immigrants.

HISTORY OF MUSLIMS AND FRANCE

Ideological Beginnings

Islam (in the most general sense) is not a newcomer in French history. Charles Martel repelled Muslim adventurers from Spain in 732 c.e. This encounter became one of the foundational myths of the French nation. French identity, and its Roman Catholic component in particular, developed as an ideological struggle against the "Saracens." The Saracens, actually Muslims from North Africa for the most part, settled in southern regions of what would become France. As the ideological storybook tells us, it took some centuries of "reconquest" to oust them. Furthermore, the Crusades, in which the Frankish kingdom was a decisive player, pitted French Christianity against Islam. However, when the Moriscos were expelled from Spain, France welcomed some one hundred thirty thousand of them to repopulate the southern provinces ravaged by the Wars of Religions. Their descendants were completely assimilated. Yet this history is somehow forgotten in the oppositional character of

"Christian" French ideology. Martel's victory was the dominant paradigm of French-Muslim encounter in the Third Republic history books.

The Algerian Conquest

The modern story of Islam in France began in 1830. At that time, French troops destroyed the piracy operating from Algiers. The United States had done the same in Tripoli in 1802, but the French endeavor soon spread beyond this limited goal. Charles X used the conquest to divert public opinion from a catastrophic domestic economic situation. To offset criticism of government politics, the French public was offered a grand scheme of conquering the Orient and showing forth the light of French civilization, and French troops ended up conquering extensive territories beyond Algiers.

Colonialism

North Africa soon became a pawn in the European competition for economic advantage through colonialism. France had to keep pace with other European states' African conquests. Besides, North Africa, especially Algeria, was very valuable in itself. Not only a convenient penal colony for prisoners of the Commune Uprising, it was near enough that the import of agricultural products was extremely profitable for the bourgeoisie of Marseille.

Algeria ultimately became three *departments* of France itself. This made Algeria, at least officially, not a colony but part of France. Although Algeria was regulated by French laws, used the French language, and employed the French educational system, it had a French governor, not a *prefect* like other French *departments*. More importantly, of course, the majority of the population was not ethnically French. Natives were treated as colonized peoples and their rights were trampled under French rule. The spoliation of lands and the pauperization of Muslim populations increased with the development of the country and the immigration of French nationals and other Europeans into Algeria. In order to prevent assimilation of Algerians into French society, Protestant missions were forbidden and later, even Roman Catholic missions, as well. If missionary efforts were successful, it was feared that the bourgeoisie would lose their grip on a cheap labor force. Meanwhile, the French military in charge of Algeria systematically strengthened the traditional Islamic leaders through bribery in the quest of pacification of the Muslim population.

Legacy of Colonialism

Ultimately, of course, the results of these policies were catastrophic. The number of the natives denied access to either freedom or the benefits of their "French" citizenship grew at an exponential rate (given the higher Algerian birth rate compared to the French), and their pathetic status eventually compelled them to violent revolution against their French overlords. Colonialism shipwrecked itself on the greedy, mediocre thinking of the merchant class. The horror of the war for Algerian independence (1954-62) is a witness to such imposture. Colonialism lived above its means and inevitably was compelled to give back what was not, in the first place, its possession.

French colonial policy, it may be argued, was instrumental in the creation of Islamist ideology. Colonial administrators attempted to manipulate believers through their leaders. As noted, the French military bought the influence of the `ulama' (religious authorities) to help pacify the Berbers. Paradoxically, this policy served to strengthen the influence of religious leaders in a population not known for its enthusiasm for religion. At the same time, many of the religious leaders "passively" opposed French influence, excommunicating those tempted to cooperate too closely with the French occupiers. In either role, the religious leaders played a significant role in the contention between French and Algerians.

PROBLEMS OF ALGERIAN IMMIGRATION

It was not until the 1980s that France became aware that it had a sizeable Muslim population that was experiencing tremendous problems stemming from its colonial heritage. Not only did Muslims enter the modern era with a negative stereotype clearly resulting from colonial and post-colonial struggles, but their colonial history and circumstances of immigration placed the majority at a severe economic and social disadvantage.

Negative International Image

The handicap of Muslims in France is not only economic and social, but is also ideological in nature. Since the 1960s the image of Islam as a religion has been distorted by biases in the media and journalistic sensationalism. As in North America the French understanding of Islam is informed by a continual flow of alleged calls to jihad, murders, and bombings. The Iranian revolution, the Lebanese civil war, the Rushdie affair, and the Gulf War coalesced public opinion in the West into fear of an awakened Islam ready to take on the world. More recently, the coup d'tat perpetrated by the army in Algeria and the desperate guerilla warfare that has continued since the cancellation of elections in which Islamist candidates were leading in 1991 have reinforced this image of Islam as the enemy of peace, always ready to take arms against the state.

Negative National Image

The negative image of Muslims in the international arena only reinforces their negative image within France itself. To begin with, immigration to France indicates the failure of the Algerian revolution. The immigrants are still patronized and their status is demeaned in the eyes of French. The legacy of the Algerian conflict still hovers over relations between French and Algerians and, by extension, other Muslims. Millions of conscripts who fought in the Algerian war for independence still harbor resentment toward those they consider their former enemies. In the popular French *imaginaire,* the tactics used by the Algerian resistance were far more barbaric than those of the ruthless French counter-guerillas. A million "Pieds Noirs" (French colonials who had settled in Algeria and considered it their home) who were "ethnically cleansed" hate Algerians. They became the victims of Algerian hatred of the French at independence in 1962; most were expelled from the country. Finally, the well publicized Algerian resistance's motto "Algeria is my country, Arabic is my language, Islam is my faith," associated Islam with the brutality of one of the cruelest guerila conflicts of this century. These events have poisoned relations among ethnic French and the Maghrebi immigrants. Indeed they favor animosity and produce a latent racism against all Muslim immigrants.

Cultural Differences

These negative images of Muslims have become the bane of the existence of the hundreds of thousands who immigrated to France to escape the desperate conditions of post-colonial North Africa. The situation is exacerbated by cultural difference between ethnic French and North African immigrants. For example, many lower class French, living cheek by jowl with Algerian immigrants in crowded slums of Paris, Marseille and Lyons complain bitterly about the Muslims' late night "breakfast" during the month of Ramadan (frequently accompanied by loud music), when the non-Muslims are trying to sleep. This may seem trivial, but is nonetheless deeply affecting the perception of thousands.

Economy and Unemployment

Most damaging to relations between the North African immigrants and the French natives, however, is economic competition. Not only do the immigrants compete with lower class French workers for jobs in a weak economy, but some immigrants have actually been able to rise to economic success, causing even greater jealousy among other French poor. For example, *l'epicerie,* the grocery, is an important part of French socialization. It is for the French females what the cafe is for the males. By the early 1980s, however, Arabs immigrants began to take over this sector of the economy. They established competitive institutions by practicing dumping (selling below cost until the competition is defeated, then raising prices to profitable levels) and almost 24-hour service, effectively outstripping the traditional French stores. The feeling of cultural and economic invasion was heightened when immigrants began to enter the cafes and hotel market as well.

Attitudes toward Religion

The high concentration of immigrants in crowded suburbs reinforces the feeling of encirclement experienced by some French. But perhaps the greatest obstacle to conviviality between the Muslim immigrants and the native French are their respective attitudes toward religion. In contrast with the great majority of the French population, religion is a central feature of communal identity for many Muslim immigrants. The French have a strong anticlerical tradition and a generally private approach to faith. Public displays of religiosity are incongruous in French society, and the avoidance of wine and pork and the practice of endogamy impede normal social relations. The overt adherence to religious rites, such as daily prayer, fasting, and exceptional dress in general set apart the immigrants. For some French, the public displays of seemingly retrograde religious fervor reinforce a feeling of spite towards both religion and its practioners.

Media Responsibility

To complicate matters, the French media dominated by the Right (*Le Figaro,* for example) are replete with negative references toward the immigrants. Phrases like the "subversion by the wombs" the "Arabic *tsunami* [tidal wave] over France," demonizing the immigrants are common. The media of the Left go to the other extreme. They frequently portray the French as intolerant, and stigmatize those who try to deal pragmatically with problems of immigration. They are therefore accused of coddling the immigrants. Thus, rather than a public dialogue on the problems of immigration, the issue is generally left to private and uninformed discourse, frequently denigrating those sympathetic to the immigrants and validating those who distrust and feel threatened by them. The latter are easy prey for an ideology promoting fascist and racist discourse, particularly that of the extreme right *Front National.*

NATIONALIST REACTION

The *Front National* and their sympathizers have been able to exploit the economic frustration of many disenfranchised French. The growing insecurity fueled by an expanding population of unemployed sons and daughters of immigrants in many suburbs has become a *leitmotiv* of the National Front's rhetoric. Rather than focus on the economic weaknesses and inept government policies that cause unemployment and insecurity, the French public is presented with a perfect scapegoat: the immigrants and, in particular, the Muslims among them. Furthermore, the Front's propaganda has been able to use rivalries among Muslims themselves, which are taken as evidence of generic Muslim violence rather than that Muslims, like all people, are not a monolithic community. Unhappily, the impression of Muslims as violent and anti-French was furthered by bombings in Paris allegedly perpetrated by obscure Muslim terrorist groups in 1986.

THE ALGERIAN GHOST

This situation was again exacerbated by the ambiguous attitude of the French government toward the anti-Islamist military junta ruling Algeria. As noted above, the Algerian military suspended the democratic process in Algeria in 1991 when the Islamist *Front Islamic du Salut* (FIS) stood on the verge of electoral success. Since that time a bloody civil war has pitted Islamists against the military government. The conflict spilled over into France when Algerians highjacked an Air France airbus, resulting in the death of four terrorists. But the worst was yet to come. A wave of subway bombings by a group associated with the Algerian *Groupe Islamique Arme* (GIA; Armed Islamic Group) resulted in the deaths of innocent French commuters. When the army was called upon to smash the Islamist guerrilla group in rural Lyons believed responsible for these bombings, it became evident in the minds of many that religion -- in particular, Islam -- is the problem with the immigrants.

Until now the majority of French have respected the *Etat de Droit* of the Republic. However, it could very well be that Islamists have made a peaceful resolution of the conflict impossible. The real danger is that if terrorist activities continue, the damaging image of a demented Islam could become normative and help the *Front National* to implant itself more deeply in the French political arena.

IDEOLOGICAL CONFRONTATION

In the remainder of this chapter I want to describe some aspects of the confrontation between the French ideology, Jacobinism, and Islamism. Jacobinism holds as essential the republican virtues of humanism, freedom, and laicism. It is a reactionary ideology, however, which from its struggle with both Catholicism and the monarchy, inherited an absolutist character. It is intolerant of any opposition, as was the king of old; it claims universal hegemony upon the conscience, as did ancient clericalism. After the birth of the Third Republic, the principle of free education was gradually implemented against the educational monopoly of the church. The official separation of church and state in 1905 consecrated the victory of laicism; it became mandatory and rabidly anti-clerical. Yet even with its hatred of religion Jacobinism could not avoid becoming the new-fashioned recipient of the hallowed. It was part of the sacral continuum only with a new foundational myth, the *Revolution*, a sacred discourse, *la morale republicaine*, a sacred space, *l'ecole republicaine*. The republican school would, with success, convert millions to the cult of the *Republic*.

CONFRONTATION OVER THE MEANING OF THE VEIL

The mounting hostility between Jacobinism and Islamism reached a crescendo in 1989 over the issue of veiling. Girls from Islamist families wore their scarves to public school. The veil was determined inappropriate by the academic authorities because it was religious dress in a public school. The children refused this interpretation and were ordered to surrender their veils. It is evident that these veils were not the only reason for such a major confrontation. More was at stake for Jacobinism. The Islamist veil invades the sacred space of the *Republic.* It refuses its morality and defies its ideology. It also responds to Jacobinism by demanding the respect of individual freedom of the believers. The veil upsets the republican order because it is considered the symbol of the Iranian revolution and the religious deprecation of the West. In French schools, the veil is seen as a constant call for rebellion against non-Muslim order. The veil also imposes a disturbing moral dilemma for the Republic. How can one let Muslim girls wear veils without creating a precedent and encouraging parents to call for secluding girls from courses and activities, if not from school altogether? Even if this liberty were granted, could the schools avoid forcing the wearing of the veil upon any girl of Muslim origin? Could the Republic dispense with equal education for girls? The average French person and the state authorities consider that everyone living in France and sending children to the schools of the Republic must accept French culture for their children. In response to this, Islamism retorts that children have rights as believers and should not be coerced on ethical and moral issues. Why force on girls coed physical education and coed school anyway? Jacobinism is thus, for the first time, confronted with an opponent who will not submit to its dictates, who, instead, uses the republican rhetoric to demand recognition of its identity and to defend public morality.

At stake for Islamism is the notion of the *ummah* (the unified Muslim community); for Jacobinism it is its alter ego, Roman Catholicism. Jacobinism refuses both the reintroduction of religious affiliation into the definition of French citizenship and the abolition of the Gallic consensus which makes irrelevant such distinctions. The Islamists' refrain, *Francais oui, musulmans aussi* ("French yes, Muslims too") contravenes French laicism. The republic desperately holds to its myths and negates the revival of religion. It seems unable to invent a compromise with religious communities as in England or the United States because its confrontational relationship to religion is still essential to its identity. It can only think in terms of domination and conflict. Until now, calls for consensus and harmonious resolution, such as the lucid proposals of Bruno Etienne, have been ignored by the authorities. Inept assessment of real difficulties with Islamism, but also with Islam in general, are still the norm among French politicians. Therefore Islam is still denied a rightful position in the legal framework of French society. Islamism is a symptom of this occultation of the second religion of France, not the harbinger of an Islamic invasion of this country.

A perfect example of this blindness toward Islam is the demise of the Kelkal group, an active guerilla cell that defied the French government in the name of Islam. What is chilling in this incident is that the young men involved were French educated. They had been raised in France. They knew the customs, the language and the history of France. What tortuous logic could have pushed them to place a bomb in the Metro?

Part of their ideology centers on the struggle for social justice in Islam. Citizens in the West have few resources to fight evils like prostitution and corruption. This means that evils, in the eyes of Islamists, cannot be defeated. Perhaps the Kelkal group believed they were helping to defeat an apparently defective political system. Perhaps they fell within the essentialist trap of blaming all individuals for the crimes of a few. Perhaps, on the other hand, they were simply expressing resentment against the society that seemed to shun them.

Whatever the specific motives of the Kelkal group, the incident points to a paradigmatic conflict between Jacobin and Islamist ideologies. Could it be that the Islamist concept of the ummah proposes a monolithic understanding of the community, a community bound by the faith and the duties associated with it? For some, this community does not know ethnic or national boundaries. The most distinctive characteristic of a Muslim would be to be Muslim before anything else. When this strict understanding of Islam is contrasted with the French secular model, which relegates religion to the private sphere and makes it only a secondary component of individual identity, the conflict is clear. Islam asks the believer to take an active part in the eradication of evil. French society strips the individual of this duty and leaves it to the state institutions.

THE BREACH OF CONSENSUS

The danger of Islamism, or the creation of social unrest by groups such as the Kelkal group, is the rupture of the religious consensus in contemporary France. This consensus delivers civil peace by ignoring the citizen's religion. Islamism assails this consensus. In the dominant French ideology, religion must stay private. Citizens must not be discriminated against on the basis of their religion, but neither should they be the given special privileges on the basis of their religion (although through subventions to religious schools, religious bodies receive indirect sponsorship from the state). The majority feel that France cannot afford to wake up its old demons. It took two centuries to relegate Roman Catholic absolutism to the private sphere. It is dangerous to leave loopholes in the relationship of the French Republic and religion. The shameful episode of Vichy (1940-44) reminds us that French citizens were discriminated against, tortured, and sent to be burned in ovens, on the basis of their religion. Moreover, Vichy policies were not only directed toward the "usual" victims of religious bigotry, the Jews. Protestants were next on the religious list. According to Bruno Etienne, Vichy allied itself with the French episcopacy to monitor Protestant communities, for the collapse of the Republic in 1940 had provided the temptation for one religion to revert to the role of a state religion.[1] This is the background of French secular revulsion at a conspicuous display of religious symbols and privilege given to any religion.

Furthermore, the majority feel that French secularism is the healthiest for Muslims. In the long run, it is the system that will give them religious freedom and civil peace. By respecting the laic principle and becoming obedient citizens of the Republic, they will be protected from religious discrimination. The French government must allow the organization of a French Islam on the model of the Protestant and Jewish system of consistories. Muslims, for their part, must make it clear that their Islamic schools and mosques are not centers of revolutionary political activity, as the public sentiment of working class France sees them. They must make it clear that wearing a veil and demanding the right to private prayer on the job are not demands for special treatment under French law, but simply different expression of private religious belief, like the Jews' yarmulke and the Christians' Christmas or Easter holidays.

---

[1]Marc Boegner, *The Long Road to Unity: Memories and Anticipations.* Tr. R. Hague (London: Collins, 1970):167, 389-90.

Further Reading:

Arkoun, Mohammed, *Rethinking Islam.* Boulder: Westview Press, 1994.

Bastenier, Albert and Felice Dassetto, eds., *Immigration et Nouveaux Pluralismes: Une Confrontation de Societes.* Bruxelles: De Boeck-Wesmael, 1990.

Boulares, Habib, *Islam: The Fear and the Hope.* London: Zed Books Ltd., 1990.

Castle, Stephen with Heather Booth and Tina Wallace, *Here for Good: Western Europe's New Ethnic Minorities.* London: Pluto Press, 1987.

Etienne, Bruno, *France et L'Islam.* Paris: Hachette, 1989.

-----, *L'Islam en France: Islam. Etat et Societe.* Paris: Editions du Centre National de la Recherche Scientifique, 1991.

Graham, Fuller, E. *A Sense of Siege: The Geopolitics of Islam and the West.* Boulder: Westview Press, 1995.

Jorgen, Nielsen S., *Muslims in Western Europe.* Edinburgh: Edinburgh University Press, 1995.

Kepel, Gilles, *Banlieues de l' Islam.* Paris: Editions du Seuil, 1987.

-----, *The Revenge of God.* University Park: Pennsylvania State University Press, 1994.

Klaus, Ferdinand and Mehdi Mozaffari, *Islam: State and Society.* Riverdale, Maryland: Riverdale Company, 1988.

Krone, Ronald E., *International Labor Migration in Europe.* New York: Praeger Publishers, 1979.

Lamand, Francis, *L'Islam en France: Les Musulmans dans la Communaute Nationale.* Paris: Albin Michel, 1986.

Leveau, Remy, and Gille Kepel eds., *Les Musulmans dans la Societe Francaise.* Paris: Presses de la Fondation Nationale des Sciences Politiques, 1988.

Power, Jonathan, *Migrant Workers in Western Europe and the United States.* New York: Pergamon Press, 1979.

Stora, Benjamin, *L'Algerie en 1995: La Guerre, l'Histoire, la Politique.* Paris: Editions Michalon, 1995.

Tibi, Bassam, *Islam and the Cultural Accommodation of Social Change.* Boulder: Westview Press, 1990.

Chapter 4

COMMEMORATIONS AND IDENTITIES:
The 1994 Tercentenary of Islam in South Africa*

Shamil Jeppie

Nineteen ninety-four was a full year for a section of South Africa's Muslim population; for many Muslims in the city of Cape Town 1994 was an unforgettable and extraordinary one. They commemorated what appeared on the shores of the city, and by imaginative extension, what affected the whole country, three centuries earlier. Shaykh Yusuf of Macassar arrived at the Cape of Good Hope in the newly created Dutch colony in 1694 as an exile and prisoner of the Dutch East India Company. The Shaykh had a relatively agreeable few years as an exile (from 1694 until his death in 1699), for he was given a state stipend and his two wives and entourage of children, slaves, imams, and servants accompanied him.

Shaykh Yusuf was no ordinary exile; he had been a religious official at the court in Bantam, and had militarily contested Dutch forces who sided with a rival of his royal patron. In his rural banishment, sixty miles northeast of the emerging colonial settlement at the Cape, he created the first Muslim community in the region. In later years this embryonic community grew as more slaves and exiles were brought to the Cape, and as converts were won over to the new faith. In this way an indigenous, creole Islam evolved.[1]

So in 1994 the Muslims of the city celebrated and commemorated the venerable Shaykh's arrival, his coming to establish their religion at the southern tip of Africa.

This essay explores the politics of this festival, arguing that it was much more than an ordinary commemorative phenomenon. A host of events and interests inserted it into identity politics and specifically into elaborating upon a Malay ethnic identity. The wider South African political context impressed itself on the festivities. The symbolism of its coincidence with the country's first open democratic elections was not overlooked by the organizers. Thus, in addition to being an occasion for memorializing a great figure, it also provided an opportunity for making political claims about Muslims and the country's future. Furthermore, it became more than an organic local celebration or even a statement about the future when the participation of southeast Asian Muslim nations began affecting the character of the event. In the end then, it was a distinctive ethnic Islam promoted by a small minority within a broader minority religious community which was celebrated in 1994.[2]

IMAGINING A COMMON HISTORY

The commemoration went beyond honoring the memory of the mythologized figure of the founder of Islam at the Cape. It was to encompass the entire three centuries-long history of Islam in this part of the continent. For the three hundred years a grim narrative of marginality, exclusion, and bondage, terminating with the fall of Apartheid, was emphasized. "We want to develop a healthy consciousness in our community for the struggle of our pioneers....[T]heir unflinching Iman never waivered and they endured the cruel sufferings of slavery to remain Muslim," the inaugural official bulletin of the organizing committee declared.[3] However, more than an exercise in public nostalgia or collective memory stirring, the festivities attempted to turn the Muslim mind to the future. "Development" -- with all the connotations of progress and modernity, and nation-building -- became a term intimately attached to the Shaykh Yusuf tercentenary project. The organizers combined nostalgia and utopian rhetoric. New opportunities and fresh beginnings bacame linked to past initiatives.

"The tricentenary is development oriented" stressed the second Tricentenary broadsheet, continuing, "We want to provide the stimulus for the development of the latent talents within the Muslim community, so that Muslims could take their rightful place in all spheres of human endeavour in this country."[4] Furthermore, the community was said to have a right to be in a jubilant mood and make good on this new moment in the country's history, because it shared a past of discrimination and subjugation with the majority of the black people whose day has finally arrived.

In the short history of modern South Africa, 1994 was to bring an end to decades of political exclusion, legal discrimination, and systematic denial of basic human rights to the indigenous peoples of the country. The creation of the South African state rested on the foundations of colonial conquest followed by the exploitation of black labor and the systematic exclusion of blacks from all sources of authority. In response there emerged a host of local and national, spontaneous and organized forms of opposition and resistance.[5] In 1990 a series of discriminatory laws were repealed and, more significantly, Nelson Mandela was released and formerly proscribed oppositional organizations were unbanned. The oldest liberation movement -- the African National Congress (ANC) -- is the best known and was also the most prominent inside the country. A process of negotiation and constitutional talks was initiated among the white ruling class and representatives of the popular resistance groups. Four years later, on 27 April 1994, the first non-racial, multi-party, free elections were held in the country and Nelson Mandela became the first president of the new South Africa.[6]

The South African state, territorially and constitutionally, only came into being and became recognized as it is today by the 1910 Act of Union. Of course, it was a union between Afrikaans- and English-speaking whites with the black majority effectively excluded and subordinated. But because Dutch colonization of the Cape region began in 1652, later official Nationalist Party mythology about the birth of a "civilized" South Africa posited this as the beginning of South African "history."[7] Thus, as a response, the false notion of more than 300 years of racial oppression and minority rule emerged. It has had a good deal of currency in popular oppositional discourse and thus amongst many black South Africans generally.[8] So in many a mind 1994 signalled the end of more than three centuries of injustice. But this popular understanding of the past undervalues the existence of independent states and societies in the interior against which successive Dutch and British colonists and colonial armies had to battle extensively before they were fully and finally subjected to colonial domination.[9]

Colonization may have begun in 1652 but its victory was not predestined, nor were its spatial limits a forgone conclusion. Even by the late nineteenth century the shape of the South African map was far from clear. But the notion of "three hundred years" of oppression is a topos which cannot easily be dispelled.

The tercentenary of Cape Islam and the end of more than "three hundred years of minority rule" was a tidy and valuable coincidence which was not lost on the organizers of the festivities. The parallel narratives of Muslim subordination since even before their arrival, indeed their very landing premised on colonial domination and resistance, on the one side, and on the other, the long dark night of white minority rule over the black populace made useful publicity for Muslims and the Tricentenary. It aligned them discursively and imaginatively with the authentic and victorious historical forces at the appropriate moment, even though it transgressed all historical complexity and factuality. The "good" side of the communal past was resurrected and narrated in broad, vague terms lest specific and contentious issues or personalities became the subject of unnecessary debate. That not all Muslims or all Muslim leaders throughout this period were opponents of racial discrimination and exploitation and supporters of black liberation, for instance, did not now matter. The organizers, as public historians, scripted a consensus Islamic narrative.

DETERMINING AN ETHNIC IDENTITY
While this "Three Hundred Years of Islam in South Africa" was ostensibly a commemoration of the founder of Islam at the Cape, and at the same time the history of Muslims nationwide, the whole event and all its festivities were located in the greater Cape Town area. The official logo for the celebrations, interestingly, was not

Cape Town's favorite symbol Table Mountain. It consisted of a map of South Africa over which Shaykh Yusuf's tomb was prominently situated with a "300 years" banner above all this. But despite this iconographic statement, the commemoration effectively ignored and suppressed the history of the more recent South Asian, Zanzibari, and other African Muslims in the western Cape and the northern provinces of the country. Cape Town was the locus of the entire celebration, despite enthusiastic talk early on about commemoration committees in the North. There were no active festival committees elsewhere in the country, no parades, rallies, exhibitions and re-creations of the history of the community.[10]

The early history of Cape Islam quite simply does not matter in the rest of the country, it would appear. The heroic figure for many Muslims in the North, their Shaykh Yusuf, is Soofie Saheb who arrived in Natal province in 1895, and apart from "establishing" the religion he is remembered for his welfare activities there. The upcoming commemoration of his arrival went virtually unnoticed outside the Natal region, and it did not seem to have mattered to the Tricentenary planners to include this figure in their version of South African Islamic history.[11] However, the entire year-long celebration was initiated and executed as if it would be, and actually already was, a national event shared across a nation's space and in temporal simultaneity. Such engineering which would evoke feelings of belonging and participation -- altogether, at the same time -- is essential in the production of a sense of national community and identity, if not of nationhood in this case.

At times the impression was created that it was even an international, global and *ummah*-wide commemoration. But the purportedly national, communal and collective experience was an immense exaggeration. In fact it was a very local, very exclusive, and thus peculiarly urban-centered Western Cape event. Moreover, despite its narrowly regional focus, the substantial community of Cape Muslims from the "Indian" residential areas who have stronger ties to South Asian expressions of Islam than to those represened by Shaykh Yusuf, was hardly incorporated into the festivities.

What stands out in this regional emphasis of the commemoration are the elaborations of strong local Malay ethnic themes; a revived Malay identity pervaded a fair number of the festival's activities and was unmistakeably part of the most significant events. Cape Town has been the site for the articulation of a spurious discourse of Malay identity since the middle years of the nineteenth-century.[12] Successive administrations in the colony attributed a fixed "Malay" ethnic label on the Muslims despite the highly heterogeneous origins of the Muslim population. Cape Town's "original" Muslims came from a variety of regions in the Indonesian archipelago, South Asia -- specifically Bengal -- and even West and East Africa.[13]

The idea of a definitive and original Malay background found its Muslim proponents among politically conservative Muslim elites in the twentieth-century. It inevitably found its white folklorists and ethnographers as well, most notably I. D. du Plessis, devoted to preserving aspects of the supposedly vanishing Malay culture, customs, language and so on. This separate national origin for the Muslims served excellently ruling class racialistic arguments and the development of segregationist policies -- with their divide and rule rationale -- which became the fully-blown Apartheid from the late 1940s onwards.[14]

There is no "traditional" or original model of Cape Muslim "manners and customs." Much less did such a paradigm and way of life reflect the nebulous and fictional "Cape Malay identity." The Tricentenary organizers, however, at times consciously and sometimes unconsciously perpetuated ideas of a timeless and pure Muslim traditon and culture at the Cape. Moreover, they helped to valorize the notion of a palpable Malay ethnic community at the tip of Africa. Muslims in the Cape, obviously, have had some definite and distinctive ways of living and doing things, but they have also changed and adapted to changes over time. A timeless, unique, and uncontaminated pre-modern simple lifestyle never existed.

However, at the arts and crafts exhibition held at the Castle of Good Hope in 1994, the artifacts on display were meant to convey images of Muslim material culture without any sense of temporality, of modification and mutation over time, and without any explicit acknowledgement of the hybrid, mixed nature of local Islamic "traditional" art, crafts, and customs. The castle was constructed by the first Dutch colonists and became a symbol of white minority rule, and thus the venue itself was steeped in colonial symbolism which was on the occasion of the Tricentenary for the first time opened for use by members of the unenfranchised majority.[15]

While there was little in the way of overt advertisement of the specious Malay character regularly attributed to local Muslim activities, there was a measure of acknowledgement of the ethnic "otherness" of the Muslims, and this exoticism assumed the dominant understandings of "Malayness." Among the attributes assigned to Muslims as Malays since the two became synonomous in the nineteenth century have been those of obedience, fidelity to the "manners and customs" of their forefathers, innate craftsmanship, that they are happy singing folk, and such standard fictions. The exhibition at the castle, which was a transgressive step into what had been until then at once white minority terrain and symbolic property, was ironically also a conservative affirmation of stereotyped ethnic identity in the sphere of material culture and practice. The exhibiton of "typical" Islamic material culture was only one of a much larger set of activities which reiterated Malay ethnicity.

CULTURAL BORROWING

Whereas this instance was an attempt to lay claim to some kind of ethnic authenticity, there were other events which undermined this claim, in addition to saying much else. The language of contemporary Islamic revivalism, for instance, was articulated fairly consistently from among the powerful assertions of organic community identity. For example, a focal point of the series of events which made up the Tricentenary was a mass rally on April 2 at the Good Hope Center, the largest conference center in the city. The actual opening of the rally was prefaced by a mass march to the venue from District Six, an area from which many Muslim and other black families were forcibly removed by Apartheid legislation from the middle 1960s, and thus a symbol both of the hated racist system and opposition to it. Indeed, processions and rallies themselves were two staples in the arsenal of tactics used by populist organizations in opposition to Apartheid. Muslim revivalist movements in Cape Town also employed these public gestures in their protests against the government.[16] The procession and rally for the Tricentenary, therefore, were not signs of timeless local "tradition" but of a much more recent phenomenon.

Furthermore, the participants were all requested by the organizers to dress in white -- women in full white *hijab* and men in white *jubbas*. Public appearance in such apparel is also a recent innovation, of the last fifteen years, among sections of Cape Town's Muslims. It reflects very contemporary influences -- local imitations and adaptations based on photographic images, of Teheran 1979, or actual experiences of young pilgrims on mount Arafat during the *Hajj*. While the mass of participants were thus dressed -- or at least were requested to cover themselves in specific "Islamic" ways, inside the meeting hall, on the podium, a completely different spectacle was produced. This brings us to the international dimension of the festivities.

The invited guests were clothed in their respective "national costumes." But the most prominent locals presiding over proceedings appeared in unmistakeably Malaysian outfits; not inventions of what was thought to have been the attire of a eighteenth-century Muslim or a nineteenth-century imam, for instance, but the foreign, Malaysian iconic half *sarong* made of deep shiny and colorful fabric, and distinctive *songkok* head-gear. This was "Malaysian national dress" which no local has ever worn. As a "national dress" it is, of course, itself a selective, political, and rather late, official fabrication of tradition and fashion in Malaysia. But whatever the case, there was absolutely no difference in the appearance of the visiting Malaysian dignitary and leading members of the organization responsible for the Tricentenary.

This was not only in stark contrast to the thousands of ordinary Muslims out in the stands in their characterless all-white outfits, as prescribed by the organizers, but it was so thoroughly new and different, and so distinctively "Malaysian" that in one moment, symbolically, the event appears as if it was indeed scripted to lead the Muslims back to their imaginary Malay origins and educate them in their true Islamic heritage and Malay tradition. Indeed, the representative of the Malaysian government, Defense Minister Datuk Seri Mohamed Najib Tun Haji Abdul Razak, in his spirited speech spoke of the Muslims rightly rediscovering their roots. On another occasion he welcomed Muslims back to the Malay fold. Nelson Mandela, whom the majority of South Africans would elect as president only a few weeks later, was also present on the front podium but he got none of the applause and enthusiastic welcome accorded to the Malaysian spokesman. Mandela, on the contrary, was jeered by a section of the crowd, in all probability supporters of the two shady Muslim political parties who had registered to contest the impending national and regional elections.

That such a warm invitation back to the "Malay world" was so well received reflects residual elements of the hegemonic discourse of the segregationist and Apartheid state which created a separate category -- that of Malay -- in the odious racial classification hierarachy of the country. In terms of the Population Registration Act of 1950, "Malay" was used as a legal state-recognized population grouping as distinct from "Coloured." The enthusiastic reception afforded the Malaysian dignitary also reflects the response of people who were in virtually total isolation during the Apartheid years. Suddenly they got hailed as lost brothers; and the hailing came with confidence from a charismatic representative of a country represented in the media as an emergent regional economic power. At least some leading members among the planners were thoroughly seduced by the attractive power of the contemporary Malaysian state and its promotion of Malay identity. The popular historian of Cape Town's Islamic past, Achmat Davids, for example, who had previously been more circumspect about the notion of Malays at the Cape, grew ever more enchanted by it. Months after the festivities he would openly declare, "When we discovered each other, there was total amazement on both sides that the culture had been so well preserved in South Africa....There is a lot of curiosity among Malays in Cape Town about Malaysia and many people are interested in discovering their roots there."[17] Here Davids is speaking without reservation about the "Malays of Cape Town," something he had not done before; instead he had himself coined the more inclusive "Cape Muslim" in his published work.[18]

The Malaysian "reclaiming" of Cape Muslims could itself usefully be recast, firstly, in the internal ethnic politics of Malaysia, and secondly, in the Southeast Asian geopolitics of identity. As I noted earlier, the entire question of Muslim ethnic origins in South Africa, barring those with incontrovertable South Asian roots who had arrived with the inflow of immigrant labor during the 1860s, is an issue fraught with problems. There are so many influences at the Cape it makes easy statements and choices of "genuine" affiliation hard and complex; there are Bengali traces, Ottoman connections, Javanese fragments, a host of diverse Arab ties, East African links, indigenous Khoisan roots, as well as Welsh and English converts, and so on. The contentious Malaysian government appropriation of the Muslims of Cape Town as lost Malays should be seen in the context of internal ethnic politics in Malaysia itself.

The Malaysian Muslim leadership has been dealing with its economically powerful non-Muslim Chinese population by using every conceivable technique of mobilizing ethnic and religious pride and resources. In recent years Muslim economic power has blossomed considerably, contributing immeasurably to their confidence and influence. *The Malay Dilemma*, title of a widely read book written in the 1970s by current Prime Minister Mahathir bin Mohamad, is on the way to being solved. The notion of a "Malay diaspora" into which it can dip for support has a valuable salutary role.[19] In this way, because of low Malay population growth and therefore a continuing and tenuous population balance with the Chinese, the Malay Muslims are searching out other "Malays" while simultaneously locating themselves as pivotal to this much larger trans-national Malay ethnic community. Thus, despite their hundreds of ethnic groups and as many languages, Indonesians and even Filipinos, immigrant communities overseas, and now a newly discovered Cape one, all belong together, with Malaysia deservedly at the head, where the Malays are in the throes of an ethnic, economic and cultural renaissance. *Bumiputras* and *orang melayu* (indigenous people), real or not, at home and in the "diaspora," are united under and loyal to the *tanah melayu* (land of the Malays).

This strategy will not, of course, solve any of the practical problems for the Malaysians but it does serve a salutary function to know that there is an international "Malay nation" spread out across the globe.

From the moment that it became acceptable in the international community to visit and deal with South Africa, in the months after the release of Nelson Mandela in February 1990, Malaysian officials and business people swiftly initiated contacts with Muslim organizations and leaders in South Africa, particularly Capetonians. Semi-official delegations, private visitors, students and professors, and other forms of contact went back and forth between Kuala Lumpur and Cape Town. The impressive presence of the senior government official, Minister of Defense, at the Tricentenary was thus the culmination of an intensive process of informal cultural and diplomatic communication. It must be noted, apart from these extensive contacts which were hurriedly cemented, that the Tricentenary committee received handsome monetary support from the Muslim Malaysian business community.[20] As well, later in 1994 more delegations trekked to Cape Town, most significantly a 250-strong Malaysian business delegation. Reportedly, a Cape Malaysian Chamber of Business was established that year, consisting of Muslim businessmen who in the words of one, felt that, "Malay businessmen have been discriminated against by the whites and the Indians" and it was time to change things.[21]

Shaykh Yusuf lived in a territory which is today part of the 13,000 islands making up the modern state of Indonesia, and more slaves and exiles came from parts of what is now Indonesia than the completely insignificant numbers who arrived from what is now Malaysia. Yet the Indonesians made no such extensive outreach bid; they did not push, it would appear, with the same energy "historic" or imagined ethnic connections, and consequently lost out in the silent contest for the loyalities and imaginary focus of leading sections of the Cape Muslims. Barring the permanent embarrassment of massive human rights abuse in East Timor, Indonesia Muslims and the nominally Muslim government also face none of the challenges from powerful minorities which the Malaysians have to contend with. Furthermore, while Islamic revivalism, with its discourse of global Islamic brotherhood, has a weighty presence in high offical circles in Kuala Lumpur, the same cannot be said for Jakarta, where older nationalist and personal loyalties to President Suharto still dominate elite politics. Perhaps this helps explain why the Indonesians were not as enthusiastic as the Malaysians in their support of the Tricentenary. In any case, Cape Town's Shaykh Yusuf Committee certainly benefitted from the revivalist Islamic sentiment of the Malaysian government.

There was indeed a place for Indonesia to play a role in the imagination and developing identity of the Muslims of the new South Africa. The bulletin of the Tricentenary proudly announced the formation of a Shaykh Yusuf Tricentenary Committee in faraway Indonesia. It spoke of a launch of festivies there in the city of Macassar, birth place of the Shaykh; of the participation of a leading Indonesian poet, Tawfiq Ismail; of the role of a senior Indonesian government minister, and the visit there of two South Africans linked to the Tricentenary.[22] What was not said, though, is that the vanished public memory of Shaykh Yusuf had to be resurrected from scratch by the Indonesian government and a student of the Shaykh's life and work, an Egyptian historian resident in the country. For Shaykh Yusuf had been entirely forgotten and featured in none of the nationalist mythology, standard histories, or popular culture of the Indonesians. The official Indonesian guest at the celebrations, nevertheless made some general and nebulous statements at the rally, the only thing possible under the circumstances, about how Indonesians love the Shaykh. He then confected an image of a politically-correct figure who did everything relevant to everything from Sufism to anti-colonialism; from the modern idea of human rights to the equally contemporary notion of religious freedom. At the mass meeting the presence of the Indonesian dignitary, however, was rather low-key and understated. Its neighbor, Malaysia, stole the show in distant Cape Town.

The official mouthpiece of the Tricentenary promised the participation of Muslim dignitaries from around the globe. It boasted of fabulous guests like "the Mufti of Russia, the Mufti of Turkey, and the Mufti of Bosnia." But it would appear that none showed up except for the two Southeast Asians and the secretary-general of the Organization of the Islamic Conference. There was no Turkish participation, no Bangladeshi, Indian, Pakistani, Tanzanian or Egyptian official participation. These are modern political formations, post-World War II creations of decolonization and colonial nationalisms, but so too are Malaysia and Indonesia. South African Muslims came originally from areas now within these nation-states, among others. South African Muslims, and the Muslims of the Cape in particular, have no unquestioned connection to any modern state or national community. Their affections, affinities, and affiliations are products more of secular politics and power, and *media*-ted cultural images, than any primordial linguistic, ethnic or religious bond and longing.

In any case, a good number of Muslims with the means to travel abroad now go to Malaysia; many have been and are invited there. A very tiny minority, largely young professionals, the *nouveaux riches*, and retired upper middle-class couples, in search of cheap electronic goods and kitsch oriental fabric and artwork, take package tours of Hong Kong, Singapore and Malaysia. They go to Malaysia to "test the water," and as tourists always do, to taste and experience the food. Cuisine is a key marker of identity in the ordinary consciousness, of "how like or unlike we are," of how much one culture has influenced another and so on. Achmat Davids, the ubiquitous community historian, is also a skilled cook of Cape fare, and always relies on dubious culinary similarities between a few Southeast Asian-style dishes and delicacies made at the Cape and (white, especially Afrikaner) South African cooking. Likewise, when talking of the Cape Muslim (now he would probably say Cape Malay) influence on South African cultural life he stresses certain "Cape Malay" dishes and thus its connections to the "Malay world."[23] But the use of culinary examples is a massive reduction and infantalization of the work of local cultural innovation. Furthermore, it defines "South African culture" in a totally elitist manner as meaning that which Afrikaans-speaking, and therefore mainly white, South Africans do in their kitchens in particular. The culinary traditions of the black majority are completely absent from Davids' considerations.

But to return to Muslims and their gastronomic experience in their so-called homeland, Malaysia: Capetonians are badly disappointed by the food's absolute "strangeness" and their total unfamiliarity with Malaysian cuisine. Instead, they settle for their custom in common with many other urban South Africans, depending on the class, of bread and tea, or scrambled eggs, jam with toast and instant coffee instead of a bowl of rice for breakfast, for instance, or whatever *satay* they are offered at other meals. Davids insistently and completely ignores the fact that cultures are not transported but made; they are forged in specific places and within time-frames, they change and are transformed over time. But he, more than the Shaykh Yusuf Tricentenary Commemoration Committee, promoted a notion of a timeless Malay culture transported from Malaysia and to which today's Muslims should refocus themselves, if not yet return there physically.[24] (Tourism benefitted from the Tricentenary. Malaysian Airlines lost no time during 1994 attractively displaying and advertising the value-for-money commodity that Malaysia is.) Mona Mikhail, a professor of Arabic at New York University, on a lecture tour of Malaysia during 1994 encountered touring South Africans who represented themselves as born-again Malays, and spoke avidly of their happiness at being reunited with their brothers and sisters.[25] Their Malay hosts echoed the "welcome home" the way the visiting Malaysian dignitary was told "welcome home" by some Cape Town Muslims.

CONCLUSIONS

The tercentenary celebrations of Islam in South Africa, as partial and regional as they were, coincided with the end of the last white parliament and the beginnings of a new democratic South Africa. The opening up of the world to the once pariah state has also benefitted some of the Muslims. The Tricentenary witnessed articulations of religious and ethnic ties by a section of the Muslim leadership with strong Southeast Asian Islamic nations. The elaboration of a Malay ethnic identity, however powerful and resonant with local interest groups, is but one of a range in a palimpsest of identities.

The discourses of Arab-centered Islam, through Saudi and to a lesser extent Egyptian-schooled clerisy; of South Asian Islamic traditions through the *tablighi jama`at* and seminarians educated there; even the dissenting rhetoric of offical Iranian Islam all have local representatives, and of course, an intellectual "modernism" is also present among a small highly-educated elite. Additionally, there is a range of "secular" political and cultural discourses which variously articulate with Muslim identities at other levels. One thinks of African nationalism, socialism, a range of contemporary youth sub-cultures, and feminisms, to mention a few well-known examples -- perhaps a new South Africanism as well.

As in the case of individuals, so too for groups, it is important to recognize the multiplicity of identities, the proliferation of subjectivities. Ethnic and nationalist movements tend to emphasize -- through the work of invention and imagination -- certain elements of belonging, to the exclusion of others, in their programs. They draw on language, history and the contemporary situation.[26] Similarly, Islamic revivalist movements concentrate on religious identity, eliding all other subject positions under what they produce as a flat and stable sign, Islam. They attempt to constitute a universal Muslim subject position; gender, class, ethnic, national, linguistic and historical differences do not matter in this construction of identity.[27] Difference is suppressed; the complexity of identities is reduced and rejected. Yet in spite of the strong projection of a single ethnic theme, the Shaykh Yusuf commemoration was multivocal. The ambivalent indentities produced by the Tricentenary -- Islamic, religious, secular, Malay, Malaysian, South African, Capetonian, indigenous, and so on -- were are are in evidence, not only because of the liminal moment, the end of the old and the inauguration of a "new" South Africa, in which the event happened, but because of the dynamic nature and ambivalent character of indentity. It needs constant restatement; there are always others to be displaced. This fact alone makes identity part of the political field.

After "three hundred years of Islam in South Africa," which has seen the proliferation of many ways of thinking and living Islam, it will indeed be lamentable when powerful Muslim countries pour money, as well as sectarian religious prejudices and ethnic preferences, into the comparatively open, multicultural and intellectually diverse Islamic community that the South African one has most often been. The re-articulation of Malay identity has the capacity to construct new boundaries within and around Muslims; novel discourses and practices will be introduced and insinuated as the appropriate and proper habit. There is a definite pecuniary and class element to all this as well, since overseas agencies and governments rely on local "well-placed" contacts and representatives. Thus, enterprising businessmen and other intermediaries will, sometimes cynically but often sincerely, play on common ethnic and religious ties to advance themselves.

If outside connections contribute to the well-being of all the citizens of the "new nation" through their Muslim ties, such links may perhaps be worthwhile and worth pursuing. The inclusive, democratic, egalitarian, and non-racial discourse of the progressive Muslim organizations of the 1980s should not now be forgotten. If representatives of the new-found ethnicity, with its wealthy connections, contribute to the type of isolation, insularity and belligerent communalism rampant elsewhere in the world (including Africa), they ought to be scorned and rejected by South Africa and its Muslim population.

---

* My fieldwork was carried out in 1994, almost immediately after some of the events described above. A number of Capetonians enthusiastically invited me to private video showings of the festivities; I have relied extensively upon these hours of recorded material. Kerry Ward (History, University of Michigan) gladly showed me her work-in-progress on South Africa and Southeast Asia. I benefitted from discussions with Seif al-Umam of Jakarta, Indonesia, and Shahab Ahmad (both in Near Eastern Studies, Princeton University). Muhammad Haron (Arabic Studies, University of the Western Cape) shared his material and his experiences in Malaysia with me. Dr. Tshidiso E. Maloka (History, University of Cape Town) kindly commented on a draft although I have not always followed his good advice; and the paper is the poorer for this neglect. Gigi Edross (Firestone Library, Princeton University), as always, read and reread many drafts with intelligence and care. An earlier version of this paper was presented to the annual conference of the

American Council for the Study of Islamic Societies, held at Villanova University in April 1995.   Professor Tamara Sonn graciously organized a panel and invited me participate in the meeting. This essay is dedicated to the memory of Mrs. Zahra Sampson, 1897-1991.

[1] See Shamil Jeppie, "Leadership and Loyalties: The Imams of Nineteenth-Century Colonial Cape Town, South Africa," *Journal of Religion in Africa* (forthcoming).

[2] According to the 1980 census report, the Muslim population of greater Cape Town was just under 140,000 out of a total population of around 1,150,000. See Yusuf da Costa, "Muslims in Greater Cape Town: A Problem of Identity," *British Journal of Sociology* 45/2 (1994):235-246.

[3] *Tricentenary Times,* January 1994.

[4] *Tricentenary Times,* March 1994.

[5] General and specialist accounts of all aspects of the South African past abound. See, e.g., Joshua Brown et al., Eds., *History from South Africa: Alternative Visions and Practices* (Philadelphia: Temple University Press, 1991); Leonard Thompson, *A History of South Africa* (New Haven, CT: Yale University Press, 1992); and Nigel Worden, *The Making of Modern South Africa: Conquest, Segregation, Apartheid* (Oxford: Blackwell, 1994).

[6] See Steve Friedman and Doreen Atkinson (eds.), *South African Review: Six* (Johannesburg: Ravan Press, 1994).

[7] See Ciraj Rasool and Leslie Witz, "The 1952 Jan van Riebeeck Tercentenary Festival: Constructing and Contesting Public National History in South Africa," *Journal of African History* 34(1993:447-468.

[8] During the 1952 Tricentenary celebrations of the arrival of Jan van Riebeeck at the Cape, a tract appeared entitled "Three Hundred Years," attacking official history which itself promoted an image of three centuries of the white, civilizing, presence in South Africa.

[9] Examples of strong independent states include the Ba Sotho and AmaZulu which both resisted colonization well into the nineteenth-century.   See studies in footnote 5 above, and also Paul Maylam, *A History of the African People of South Africa from the Early Iron Age to the 1970s* (Cape Town: David Philip, 1986).

[10] Despite reports of a launch of a committee in the Transvaal early in 1994 there was no subsequent news about it. See "Jhb Begins Plans for Tricentenary," *al-Qalam,* February 1994.

[11] "Celebrations Mark Centenary of Soofie Saheb," *al-Qalam,* February 1995.

[12] Vivian Bickford-Smith, *Ethnic Pride and Racial Prejudice in Victorian Cape Town* (Cambridge: Cambridge University Press, 1995).

[13] Robert C-H Shell, *Children of Bondage: A Social History of the Slave Society at the Cape of Good Hope, 1652-1838* (Hanover: Wesleyan University Press, 1994).

[14] Shamil Jeppie, *Historical Process and the Constitution of Subjects: I.D. du Plessis and the Re-invention of the 'Malay.'* Honours thesis. (Cape Town: University of Cape Town, 1987).

[15] See Kerry Ward, "The '300 Years: The Making of Cape Mulsim Culture' Exhibition, Cape Town, April 1994: Liberating the Castle?" Paper presented to the Center for African Studies Seminar, University of Cape Town, July 1994.

[16] See Shamil Jeppie, "Amandla and Allahu Akbar: Muslims and Resistance in South Africa," *Journal for the Study of Religion* 4/1 (1991):3-19.

[17] "Malaysia Rediscovers Links with SA Malays," *Mail and Guardian,* August 25-31, 1995.

[18] See for instance his *Mosques of the Bo-kaap* (Athlone, Cape Town: SAIAIR, 1979).

[19] "Rise of the Malay World," *Asiaweek,* August 1994; "Malaysia's Overweening Elite," *Guardian Weekly,* March 13, 1994.

[20] Since there were no published financial records by August 1994 I have been unable to ascertain exactly the figure. Local Muslim businesses and the Cape Town City Council were the other sources of funding.

[21] Mr. M. F. R., private interview with author, Cape Town, August 1994.

[22] *Tricentenary Times,* March 1994.

[23] See, for example, *al-Qalam,* February 1994; *Mail and Guardian,* August 25-31, 1995.

[24] *Mail and Guardian,* August 25-31, 1995.

[25] Personal communication, Professor Mikhail to author, Manhattan, April 1995.

[26] The influence on this essay of Eric Hobsbawm and Terence Ranger, Eds., *The Invention of Tradition* (Cambridge: Cambridge University Press, 1983)

and Benedict Anderson, *Imagined Communities* (London: Verso Press, 1983) should by now be evident.

[27] See Ernesto Laclau and Chantal Mouffe, "Recasting Marxism: Hegemony and New Political Movements," *Socialist Review* 12/66 (1982):96-113; and Catherine Belsey, *Critical Practice* (London: Methuen 1980).

Chapter 5

ISLAMISM AND KURDISH NATIONALISM:
Rival Adversaries of Kemalism in Turkey

Haldun Gülalp

The Kurdish question is the Achilles' heel of the Turkish state. In the 1960s and 1970s, the revolutionary Left attempted to exploit the Kurdish situation in order to mobilize separatist forces in support of their own goals. Left-wing opposition to the Kemalist state is now superseded by the Islamist movement. Islamists, too, are using the Kurdish issue in pursuit of their own goals. It appears, however, that Islamists have been more successful in this than the Leftists. One of the fundamental reasons for the recent electoral gains of the pro-Islamist *Refah* (Welfare) Party is the inability of the Turkish government to resolve the Kurdish crisis.

KEMALISM AND TURKISH NATIONALISM
The beginning of the Kurdish question in Turkey dates back to the creation of the republic under Kemal Atatürk's leadership. In a policy set in the early years of the republic, the Turkish state officially denied the existence of a distinct Kurdish ethnicity. Kurdish citizens were consequently forced to suppress their identity.

The Turkish republic was built on the ruins of the Ottoman Empire, which was defeated and occupied at the end of World War I.

The Turkish War of Liberation was essentially a continuation of the world war. At the successful conclusion of the liberation war, the Kemalist leadership dealt the final blow to the Ottoman *ancien régime* by proclaiming a republic in 1923. Since the new state was a descendant of the Ottoman Empire, Islam was originally its basis of unity. But once the republic was established, a national identity was attached to the state, denying the Islamic heritage and building a Turkish collectivity delimited by common territory. The Kemalist revolution thus forged a nation on the remnants of the Ottoman Empire.

The Islamic pillars of the state began to be demolished after the Republic of Turkey was formally established. In March 1924, the caliphate was abolished, and all members of the Ottoman dynasty were banished from the country. The Constitution of April 1924 stated that sovereignty belonged to the nation. The same constitution originally stated that the religion of the nation was Islam, but this clause was stricken in 1928. The progressive secularization of the state implied a profound change in both social identity and political legitimacy. As a result of the Kemalist revolution the state had been transformed from an Islamic empire to a national state, and its legitimizing ideology from Islam to Turkish nationalism.[1]

The basis of Kemalism was territorial nationalism. Turkey was a geographical concept, and the Turkish people were defined as those living within that territory.[2] Although formally a territorial concept, in reality Turkishness became a linguistic category. In 1925, the Kemalist regime formally denied the existence of any ethnic identities other than Turkish. This, in effect, meant that the largest linguistic minority in Turkey, the Kurds, officially ceased to exist.[3] The origin of this policy was the Turkish state's reaction to the Kurdish rebellion led by Shaykh Said. After the uprising was put down, thousands of Kurds were forcibly resettled in the western provinces of the country. From then on, a Kurdish citizen could assimilate into the Turkish mainstream but such assimilation necessitated the suppression of one's Kurdish identity.

Researchers agree that the Shaykh Said rebellion was a Kurdish nationalist rebellion in religious garb. Said was an influential and revered religious leader as the head of the Naqshbandi order, which was instrumental in organizing the uprising. He publicly condemned the Kemalist regime for destroying religion and incited rebellion to end the "blasphemy." Thus, although the objective of the leadership was to create an independent Kurdistan, or at least win autonomy, it used a religious language to motivate the followers into rebellion.[4] In addition, the British had had a longstanding interest and involvement in Kurdish nationalism. Although there was no direct evidence of British involvement in the Shaiykh Said rebellion, as far as the Kemalist regime was concerned the Kurds were in alliance with the British and were serving a sinister imperialist plan to divide up the country which the nationalist had fought so hard to save from occupation.[5]

The government quickly and forcefully responded to the rebellion, which it characterized as a "reactionary" uprising. The rebellion broke out in February 1925 and Shaykh Said was captured in April. The incident revealed the Kemalist regime's perception of an intimate connection between the Kurdish and Islamic threats to its own stability. It prompted the regime to accelerate its move towards further secularization and Turkish nationalism. Many of the "modernizing reforms" were legislated after this incident. In the following months and years the Swiss Civil Code and the Italian Penal Code were adopted, the Dress and Headgear Law and the Alphabet Law were passed, all religious orders, lodges, and shrines were closed down and outlawed.[6] The question of identity raised at the inception of the Turkish Republic was now answered by the Kemalist regime: Turkey was a unified nation aspiring to achieve Western civilization.

Particularly in the 1980s and 1990s, however, the Kemalist definition of Turkey began to be seriously challenged. In this period the protectionist welfare state was dismantled, leading to a disenchantment with the nation-state and the rise of alternative projects of community formation -- Kurdism as an intra-national ethnic identity movement and Islamism as a supra-national civilizational movement. Thus, with the erosion of confidence in the nation-state, the Kemalist project and its embedded promises came under attack specifically on two fronts. A new wave of Kurdish separatist uprising began to challenge the assumption of being a "unified nation" and the Islamist political movement began to challenge the goal of "Westernization." As we see in the rest of this chapter, these two separate threats combined in unexpected ways.

GULF WAR AND THE KURDISH QUESTION

The Kurdish uprising in the 1980s and 1990s has been led by the PKK (Kurdistan Workers' Party). The PKK is the first Kurdish nationalist movement in Turkish history that is not based on the Kurdish elite but on poor peasants and workers. Until the PKK, all Kurdish movements had been led by elites. The PKK, by contrast, represents the most marginal sections of Kurdish society. Both its leadership and members are drawn almost exclusively from the lowest social classes. In contrast to Shaykh Said, for example, PKK leader Abdullah Ocalan is the son of a landless peasant. Nevertheless, similar to the way in which Shaykh Said used Islamic ideology to mobilize Kurds for national independence, Ocalan is using Marxist ideology for the same purpose. The founding doctrine of the PKK represents Kurdistan as a "classic colony" where feudal landowners and the comprador bourgeoisie collaborate with the colonizers, and its ultimate objective is to wage an armed struggle to separate Kurdistan from Turkey.[7]

The PKK was founded in 1978 and launched its first large-scale military offensive against the Turkish state in 1984. The Turkish government fought this organization until 1991 under heavy media censorship. In accordance with the Kemalist tradition, the existence of a Kurdish resistance movement was not publicly admitted. In January 1991, however, President Turgut Ozal suddenly and unexpectedly announced that he was half-Kurdish and that he believed that the ban on the use of the Kurdish language ought to be lifted. Later that year he persuaded the parliament to pass legislation formally permitting the use of the Kurdish language for "non-political" (i.e., commercial and cultural) purposes. This was a significant move, given that the traditional form of reference to Kurds was "mountain Turks" and to unrest in the Kurdish region was the "Eastern problem." In the same year, the parliament also removed several articles of the penal code which banned political organization and propaganda along the lines of social class and religion. The articles about social class in the penal code were specifically designed to counter any "communist" threat and were notorious for restricting the freedom of thought and association for most of the Turkish republic's history. They were replaced with a ban on organization and propaganda for "separatism."

The coincidence of these two pieces of legislation can be traced to the period of the Gulf crisis. That "communism" was no longer seen as a threat does not require much comment. The Cold War had begun to wind down after Gorbachev came to power and its end was sealed by the formation of the anti-Saddam alliance at the time of the Gulf crisis. That the same incident would lead to the recognition of Kurds as a distinct ethnicity in Turkey, however, is not as self-evident and requires some explanation.

President Ozal was quick to take an active position in the anti-Saddam alliance, formed soon after Iraqis' invasion of Kuwait in August 1990, and was already expressing eagerness to take military action against Iraq in December 1990. As the mid-January 1991 deadline for Saddam to withdraw his troops from Kuwait approached, Ozal intensified his belligerent tone and declared in the national and international media Turkey's willingness and readiness to do its part. It was during the course of the U.S. bombing campaign over Baghdad in the second half of January that the ban on the use of the Kurdish language in Turkey was lifted. The connection between Ozal's declared belligerence against Saddam's regime and the unexpected and unprecedented domestic political move was duly noted by reporters in Turkey.[8] Ozal had begun to openly discuss the unfairness of the loss of the Mosul province to Iraq in negotiations with Great Britain after the Lausanne Treaty was concluded in 1923 and to raise the present possibility of a federal Turkish-Kurdish state which would reclaim that province.

In other words, President Ozal had ulterior motives in his recognition of the Kurdish minority inside Turkey. He was hoping that the U.S.-led alliance would need Turkey's help to invade Iraq in the North, and that the Turkish army would thus occupy the Kurdish part of Iraq. An eventual dismemberment of Iraq would consequently leave the Kurdish territory under Turkish control. In order to prepare the groundwork for a possible incorporation of the Kurdish territory into a greater Turkey, the government had to demonstrate the moral authority to do so. Clearly, Turkey could not be trusted if it continued to deny the existence of Kurds within its own borders.

Moreover, Ozal must also have figured that the move to incorporate the Iraqi-Kurdish territory would undercut the PKK, which was considered to be much more dangerous due to its Marxist-Leninist ideology than the Kurdish leadership inside Iraq. In fact, in a policy orientation established during the Gulf War and its aftermath, the Turkish government came to recognize the Iraqi-Kurdish leadership as allies in its anti-PKK efforts.[9]

Ozal's scenarios never came to pass; Turkey never even took any active part in the military operation against Iraq. Regardless, the genie was out of the bottle. Mention of the Kurdish question in public discourse was no longer taboo. But accepting the distinct ethnic identity of Kurds had a paradoxical effect. Previously, the problem was described as one of terrorism, and its source was never confronted. Naming the Kurds officially for the first time was equivalent to naming the enemy. Although the government was trying very hard to distinguish between Kurd and terrorist, in the eyes of many, it was Turkish nationalism against Kurdish nationalism.[10]

Bringing the Kurdish issue out into the open made it clear that the "problem" was not limited to the activities of a terrorist organization. Kurdish grievances were now being represented by other organizations as well, including a legal political party, which, however, was continually being closed down to reopen under another name. In 1991 several deputies who had entered the parliament on the Social-Democratic Populist Party ticket resigned and formed their own party, *Halkin Emek Partisi* (People's Labor Party). In 1993 the State Security Court indicted the founders of *Halkin Emek Partisi* for separatist propaganda, and the party itself was outlawed by the Constitutional Court. By then the deputies had resigned to form a new political party, Democracy Party (DEP).

In July 1993, in one of her first actions as Prime Minister, Tansu Çiller made a highly publicized agreement with the military and effectively left the "resolution" of the Kurdish issue in their hands. At every opportunity, the government made it clear that no political solution was going to be considered until "terrorism" (i.e., the armed uprising led by the PKK) was completely stamped out. This situation led to an escalation of the tension. In March 1994, the parliament voted to lift the immunity of seven DEP deputies on charges of separatist propaganda. In an embarrassing show of state force, these deputies were arrested at the doorsteps of the parliament. In June 1994 the Constitutional Court ordered DEP closed. Several of the deputies who were DEP members, but who had escaped the March arrests, fled the country. In a State Security Court trial which ended in December 1994, the arrested deputies each got up to fifteen years in prison.[11]

A few months later, on the eve of March 21, 1995, the Turkish army crossed the Iraqi border one more time to root out the PKK fighters.[12] This operation, which involved 35,000 troops and lasted five weeks, was described as the largest in history of the Turkish republic. Although the operation started on the Kurdish New Year, Newroz, which was also the anniversary of the first large-scale PKK offensive in 1984, the timing was more closely related to the agreement that Turkey had signed with the European Union, just two weeks earlier, on March 6. Its unprecedented scale, too, indicated the pressure of time put on the Turkish government by the European Union (EU). A brief examination of the broader context of this operation will illustrate the differences between the U.S. and European positions on the Kurdish issue and vis-à-vis the Turkish government.

TURKEY'S ROLE IN THE WESTERN ALLIANCE

One of Turkey's greatest fears at the end of the Cold War was that it would be shunned by its Western allies for having lost its strategic value. For a brief period between the dissolution of the Soviet bloc in the fall of 1989 and the Iraqi invasion of Kuwait in the summer of 1990, the political leadership of Turkey was casting about for alternative definitions of the country's role within the global order. With its application to join the European Community pending and unlikely to receive a favorable response, the leadership at the time was prepared to turn the country towards the East. The Gulf crisis came as a welcome opportunity for Turkey to once again demonstrate its unequivocal commitment to protect Western interests in the region.

Since the collapse of the Soviet Union and the rise of Islamist movements around the world, NATO has shifted its focus of attention from the former to the latter. This shift was already evident in the aftermath of the Gulf War, but it finally became formalized in the Brussels meeting of NATO ambassadors on February 8, 1995. In that meeting, NATO ambassadors expressed "concern about Islamic fundamentalism" and announced the beginning of "a new 'southern strategy'... for tackling instability in North Africa and the Middle East."[13]

Since the end of the Cold War the Turkish government has been using the Islamic specter, in place of the communist specter, as a threat in its dealings with Western governments. With the unexpected success of the Islamist Refah Party in the local elections of March 1994, this threat became particularly credible. Although the European Union persisted in putting pressure on the Turkish government regarding human rights violations in its handling of the Kurdish situation, Turkey's use of the Islamic threat has been effective with the U.S. administration which has come to define Turkey as the "centerpiece" of U.S. policy and interests in a "chaotic region of the world."[14]

Regarding Turkey's relations with the European Union, the U.S. position echoes the Turkish position -- that Turkey would form a nice bridge between Western Europe and the Muslim world if admitted into the European Union, but would fall into the hands of the Islamists if left out. In this reasoning, the latter option would only contribute to the deepening of the confrontation between Islam and the West. After dragging its feet for a long time, the EU reluctantly admitted Turkey into its "customs union" on March 6, 1995, subject to subsequent ratification by the European Parliament. Although it implied no commitment as to any future full membership in the EU, Turkey's admission into the customs union was greeted with enthusiasm in both Ankara and Washington.

There were clear indications that the U.S. played a part in exhorting the EU governments to accept Turkey.[15] The difference between the U.S. and European positions on Turkey became even more evident after the Turkish incursion into Iraqi territory in pursuit of PKK guerillas which followed the signing of the customs union agreement only by weeks. The agreement still had to be ratified by the European Parliament and it stipulated that Turkey pass laws safeguarding democracy and civil rights for all its citizens before the deadline of 31 December 1995. Therefore Turkey was taking a serious risk of jeopardizing the agreement with this cross-border operation.[16] But the signing of the customs union agreement had the paradoxical effect of precipitating Turkey into increased military action. Now that the Europeans had agreed to accept Turkey, the civilian government had no argument left to hold back the military, which was getting increasingly impatient. Confronted with a deadline to pass laws protecting human rights and democracy, the government could try to take advantage of this window of opportunity.[17] Under intense pressure, the Turkish government declared the operation a success and withdrew the troops within five weeks.[18]

Yet, despite all this seemingly sensitive monitoring of foreign pressures and the fine-tuning of diplomacy, the fundamental shortcoming of policy remained in place: Turkey was still treating the Kurdish question as primarily a security matter and regarded the military solution as the only conceivable one. Significantly, among the political parties in Turkey, only Refah opposed the cross-border operation.[19]

REFAH AND THE ISLAMIST POSITION ON THE KURDISH QUESTION

Refah was founded in 1983, when the first general election following the military coup of 1980 was scheduled to take place. Military rulers at that time banned Refah from contesting that vote, and the party's first contest was in the local elections in 1984. Starting with a meager 4.4 % vote in 1984, Refah steadily increased its showing in every single election since then to become a major contender for national power.[20]

Refah's rise reflects a crisis of Turkey's ruling ideology, Kemalism, which represents a project of Westernist modernization. Kemalism accepted Western civilization as the "universal" normative structure and the basis for nationalist-statist development. It involved at least a partial denial of Turkey's cultural and historical heritage in return for the promises of economic and technological advancement. By the 1980s, however, Turkey's development gap was still unclosed; its question of identity remained unresolved; and the protectionist welfare state began to be dismantled. The promises of statism, nationalism and developmentalism had failed.

With the help of a military regime installed in 1980, the Turkish development trajectory turned from a nationalist-statist strategy to a transnationalist and market-oriented one. The decline of nationalist and statist policy in this period brought about a crisis in the popular ideology which supported nationalist-statist developmentalism. The state could no longer claim the loyalty of its people. Secularist legitimation was undermined together with the collapse of the conviction that the state would deliver and that the common national interest of development would be protected.

Islamism originates from the failure of the nationalist promises of Westernization and represents a post-nationalist ideology. The nation-state in Turkey was built along the lines of the Western model. In the Islamist view, nationalism is ultimately a Western ideology and its adoption amounts to emulating the West. Far from being eradicated by modernization, Islamism has thrived in the current period of Turkey's deepened integration with global capitalism. The erosion of confidence in the nation-state has caused its supporting ideology, Kemalism, to be perceived primarily in terms of its oppressive aspects. In contrast to this, Refah has convincingly billed itself as the party of the "periphery" against the "center." Today, political opposition in Turkey to such widespread social ills as poverty, unemployment, corruption and the like is represented primarily by Refah which has successfully tapped into popular disillusionment with the unfulfilled and impossible promise of "catching up with the West" by following in its footsteps.

Kemalist circles still consider Islamism a traditionalist movement bound to disappear with industrialization and urbanization. Yet, unlike in the 1970s, when Islamism was a political movement based on the petty bourgeoisie of provincial towns, Refah's constituency now includes members of the young professional middle class, students, and a large marginalized and dispossessed population in the metropolitan centers. Therefore, in the current period, the constituency of political Islam includes social segments which are likely to grow rather than shrink. The Kemalist position misses the real sources of Islamist strength in contemporary Turkey: its populist radicalism and its representation of the need for change.

The three issues most representative of Refah's political philosophy are its call for the establishment of a "just economic order," the proposal for a political system with "multiple legal-orders" and its position on the Kurdish question.[21] According to Refah leaders, the "just economic order" is based on the Islamic principle of justice. Its goals include spiritual development, protection of the environment, elimination of corruption, decentralized administration, promotion of individual enterprise, and withdrawal of the state from all economic activities. In this economic model the state deals only with infrastructure and maintaining order. Hence, the leaders claim, Refah holds a commitment to private initiative and entrepreneurship. Refah is critical, however, of "usurer capitalism" as an exploitative system run by "imperialists and Zionists," and of their organization, the IMF, which pursues "neo-colonialist" policies through its austerity measures. Refah proposes that, instead of trying to join the European Community, Turkey should initiate an Islamic Common Market.[22]

Regarding political structure, Refah proposes a system of "multiple legal-orders" and the freedom of individuals to live by that legal-order which corresponds to their beliefs. Refah considers this an appropriate constitutional amendment to the principle of secularism. The proposal derives from the Islamist argument that in Islam the community takes priority over the state. Hence, "democracy," the rule of majority over the minority, should be replaced with "pluralism," whereby each community is governed by its own belief system. In a given society, several different legal systems may thus coexist.   The role of the state would be to guarantee the autonomy of each community, and the laws and conventions of each community would be binding for all its members.[23]

Finally, regarding the brutal and fruitless confrontation of Kurdish and Turkish nationalisms, Refah opposes both the PKK and the Turkish government and offers a platform of unity between Turkish, Kurdish and other ethnic groups on the basis of Islam. Refah proposes official recognition of a distinct Kurdish ethnic identity and freedom of linguistic and cultural expression. Islamists blame the rise of the PKK on Kemalism on the following grounds. First, the PKK has only gained popularity among the Kurdish people because of the oppressions of the Kemalist regime.   Secondly, and more importantly, the foreign idea of nationalism was introduced to our society by Kemalism; and now the Kurds are using that same ideology.   According to Islamists, just as the Ottoman Empire disintegrated due to nationalism, so the current situation may lead to the disintegration of the Turkish Republic.[24]

Refah's position of transcending both nationalisms has drawn reaction from both sides.   Mainstream media accuse Refah of pandering to the PKK, while pro-PKK circles characterize it as the secret arm of Turkish capital working to undermine the revolutionary struggle of the Kurdish people. But, in fact, Refah offers an alternative to those Kurds who are disaffected by the Turkish state but are not inclined to follow the PKK. This is doubtless an important factor in Refah's popularity in the Kurdish provinces. Although in the nation-wide local elections of March 1994 a significant portion of the voters in the southeastern provinces abided by the boycott called by the (pro-Kurd) Democracy Party (according to DEP estimates, this exceeded 50 % in certain areas), most of those who did go to the polls voted for Refah. Since both DEP and Refah reject the Kemalist state and its ideology of Turkish nationalism, given DEP's boycott of the elections, Refah may have attracted some DEP votes as the only alternative opposed to Kemalism. But, in addition, Refah seems to have attracted the votes of those who reject both the Turkish nationalism of the government and the Kurdish nationalism of the PKK.[25]

In a more immediate context, Refah has long been critical of the government's policy on Iraq. Indeed, it has been the most vocal of all political parties in Turkey to oppose the U.S.-led embargo on Iraq as well as the foreign military presence on Turkish soil in the context of operation "poised hammer." The embargo, in particular, has had a devastating effect on the Kurdish region's economy and contributed to the depopulation of the region on top of the forced depopulation policies of the government. Although over the years the Turkish government has begun to waver on its support of the embargo and attempted to put pressure on the U.S. to let Iraqi oil flow through the Turkish pipeline, it has never reached the point of defying the West, which is precisely what Refah advocates.

FEAR OF ISLAM

Fear of an Islamic government in Turkey seems to be the driving force of United States policy. The U.S. government may, in the final analysis, even be counting on the Turkish military against such an eventuality. This may explain why the U.S. has readily supported the Turkish military in its handling of the Kurdish issue and defended the Turkish side against the European allies. The notion of relying on the military to fend off an Islamic threat, however, is highly misguided. Such an option would not only fail in its objectives and deepen the polarizations in society, as military interventions routinely tend to do, but it would also mean a lost opportunity to moderate the Islamist movement in Turkey. Refah has demonstrated a capacity to function within the procedural framework of a democratic regime and even move into the mainstream in order to expand its electoral base. Denying Refah an opportunity would only serve to strengthen the hand of the more extremist elements within the Islamist movement.

The fear of Islam is also used to build a case for Turkey's entry into the EU, despite opposition by European governments which complain about Turkey's human rights violations in its handling of the Kurdish issue. Yet it is not clear how Turkey's entry into the customs union would weaken the Islamist opposition or somehow contribute to stopping Refah from coming to power. The customs union does not involve any serious concessions on the part of

Europe. For example, it does not provide for the free movement of Turkish labor. Its likely impact would be to bring Turkey closer into the European economic orbit which might in turn tie the hands of an Islamic government. For this reason, Refah leaders have declared that they will tear up the customs union agreement first thing when they come to power.[26] Non-Islamist circles in Turkey, however, unrealistically regard the customs union agreement as a first step toward full integration with the EU.

The case for Turkey's entry into the EU is also based on a flawed reasoning. According to an oft-repeated argument, recently communicated to the U.S. public by Prime Minister Tansu Çiller,[27] Turkey is the only secular and democratic Muslim country in the world and, as such, presents a powerful alternative to the Iranian model. She suggested that if Turkey is rejected by Europe, Turkey would be tempted to reject Europe in return and opt for an Islamic regime. The flaw in this assertion is that if Turkey is admitted into the European Union it would cease to be a model for other Muslim countries. Since these countries will not, and could not, become members of the European Union or any other such Western alliance, they will find themselves in the same situation that Turkey is supposedly trying to escape: having been left outside, they will be tempted to opt for the Iranian model.

The polarization of Turkish domestic politics now hinges on the Kurdish question. With DEP or any other pro-Kurdish party unable to function without harassment, Refah has emerged as the primary recipient of the Kurdish vote and hence, by default, as the sole representative of the Kurdish population. The ongoing crisis in the Kurdish region of Turkey is also exacerbated by the unresolved status of Iraq's territorial integrity due to the continued standoff between Saddam's regime and the United States. Since the conclusion of the Gulf War the U.S. government has left the region in turmoil, and chosen to let internal struggles run their course, while seeking more short-term goals such as controlling the flow of oil out of the region. The oil embargo on Iraq as well as the military operations against the PKK have cost Turkey countless billions of dollars over the years. The contribution of these costs to the economic crisis and the overall sense of chaos in the region have led to a generalized social opposition which is successfully appropriated by Refah. The Iraqi-cum-Kurdish turmoil, partly created and left in suspension by Western powers, has proven to be a tremendous boost to the popularity of Refah which campaigns on a platform of defying the West. The continuation of the Kurdish crisis only serves to strengthen Refah.[28]

---

[1]See Sherif Mardin, "Religion and Secularism in Turkey," Ergun Ozbudun and Ali Kazancigil, Eds., *Ataturk: Founder of a Modern State* (London: Hurst, 1981).

[2]See Enver Ziya Karal, "The Principles of Kemalism," Ergun Ozbudun and Ali Kazancigil, op. cit..

[3]Because Turk and Kurd are not racial categories, there is no visible marker other than language to distinguish one from the other.

[4]See Martin van Bruinessen, *Agha, Shaikh and State* (Utrecht, 1978); Mete Tuncay, *Turkiye Cumhuriyeti'nde Tek Parti Yonetiminin Kurulmasi: 1923-1931* (Ankara: Yurt Yayinlari, 1981); Robert Olson, *The Emergence of Kurdish Nationalism and the Sheikh Said Rebellion, 1880-1925* (Austin: University of Texas Press, 1989).

[5]Tuncay, *Turkiye,* loc. cit., pp. 130-31; Olson, *Emergence,* loc. cit., pp. 124-33.

[6]Tuncay, *Turkiye,* loc. cit., pp. 149-73; Olson, *Emergence,* loc. cit., pp. 158-59.

[7]See Martin van Bruinessen, "Between Guerilla War and Political Murder: The Workers' Party of Kurdistan," *Middle East Report* 18/4 (July/August 1988):40-46.

[8]In particular, by the prominent columnist Guneri Civaoglu. See his articles in *Sabah,* 27 January and 2 February 1991.

[9]See *New York Times,* 9 December 1994.

[10]Sengun Kilic, *Biz ve Onlar: Turkiye'de Etnik Ayrimcilik* (Istanbul: Metic Yayincilik, 1993).

[11]See *New York Times,* 9 December 1994.

[12]Since the creation of a power vacuum in northern Iraq at the end of the Gulf War in 1991, the PKK had been able to establish military bases outside the Turkish border and the Turkish government had launched several limited military operations across the Iraqi border to remove those PKK bases.

[13]*Financial Times,* 9 February 1995.

[14]As stated by Assistant Secretary of State Richard Holbrooke in a National Public Radio interview, 12 April 1995.

[15]Already in a statement made on 20 February 1995, President Suleyman Demirel had anticipated Turkey's admission and contended that recent developments in Algeria had had a profound impact on Western thinking about Turkey's role in the region (*Hurriyet,* 21 February 1995). Demirel made this statement during a visit to Turkey by Assistant Secrtary of Richard Holbrooke. Holbrooke himself held a press conference the next day before departing from Ankara to express his government's support for Turkey's admission into the customs union and his belief that human rights violations in Turkey were not at an extreme point (*Milliyet,* 22 February 1995).

[16]As expected, the United States came to Turkey's support, while the European governments condemned Turkey's action (*The New York Times,* 29 March 1995, 7 April 1995.)

[17]In the summer of 1994, exactly one year after her coming to power and handing over the Kurdish issue to the military, Prime Minister Tansu Ciller declared that the military phase of the struggle was over. She said that the time had come to begin the economic phase of the struggle and develop the Kurdish region to undermine PKK's popularity. It soon became clear, however, that the military conflict was far from over. The army was still eager to go inside Iraqi territory and finish the PKK off. From the government's point of view, if this was going to be done it had better be done quickly.

[18]There have been several other cross-border operations since then, though none on the same scale.

[19]*Cumhuriyet,*   22 March 1995.

[20]See Haldun Gulalp, "Islamist Party Poised for National Power in Turkey, *Middle East Report* 25/3-4 (May-August, 1992):54-56.

[21]The discussion in the rest of the section draws on Gulalp, ibid.

[22]Necmettin Erbakan, *Adil Ekonomik Duzen* (Ankara, 1991).

[23]Ali Bulac, *Islam ve Demokrase* (Istanbul: Beyan Yayinlari, 1993).

[24]Abdurrahman Dilipak, "PKK Kemalizmden Guc Almaktadir," Mehmed Ali Soydan, ed., *Turkiye'nin Refah Gercegi* (Erzurum: Birey Yayincilik, 1994):262-63.

[25]Ali Bulac, *Cumhuriyet,* 24 April 1994.

---

[26]*Cumhuriyet,* 7 March 1995.

[27]MacNeil-Lehrer interview, PBS, 18 April 1995.

[28]We may note the following events that have taken place since this paper was completed in December 1995: On December 13, 1995, the European Parliament voted to ratify Turkey's inclusion into the customs union but noted that it would be vigilant against any human rights violations. On December 24, 1995, early general elections took place in Turkey. Refah emerged as the largest party but did not win enough seats in the parliament to form a majority government by itself. Its efforts to form a coalition government also proved fruitless due to pressure from anti-Refah forces on its potential coalition partner, the Motherland Party. Motherland instead joined with Tansu Çiller's True Path Party to form a minority coalition, which was supported from outside by Bülent Eçevit's Democratic Left Party. Çiller stepped down as prime minister and was replaced by Mesut Yılmaz, the leader of Motherland. The minority coalition with outside support was put together as a broad-based front to stop Refah from coming to power. At this time (April 1996), political instability in Turkey continues, as does the military conflict with PKK. [As of July 1996, Refah has joined a coalition with Ciller's True Path Party and Refah leader Necmettin Erbakan has become prime minister, approved by a narrow margin in the Turkish parliament. Turkey's agreements with the West remain in place. -Ed.]

About the Contributors

Haldun Gülalp, assistant professor of sociology at Bogaziçi University in Istanbul, holds doctoral degrees in economics from Ankara University and in sociology from Binghamton University in New York. He has published widely on social and political change in Turkey.

Abdul Hadi Hoffmann, international consultant for the Bonn-based MediaCompany, has conducted seminars on public relations in Europe, the Middle East, and Central Asia, as well as for UNICEF. He is author of *Die Neue Soziale Frage und die Zukunft der Demokratie* (The New Social Question and the Future of Democracy; Bonn, 1976), *Die gelenkte Gesellschaft* (The Planned Society; Bonn, 1977), *Al-Murshad ila al-Hizb al-Siyasiyyah* (Guide to [the Work of] Political Parties; Amman, 1995), and *Zwischen allen Stuhlen: Ein Deutscher wird Muslim* (Between the Stools: A German Becomes Muslim; Bonn, 1995).

Shamil Jeppie holds a Ph.D. from Princeton University, and is a Mellon fellow at the American University of Beirut. He has published several articles on popular culture in the Western Cape region of South Africa, in such journals as the *Journal of Religions in Africa* and the *Journal for the Study of Religion*.

Michel Machado, a native of France, is a graduate student in Religious Studies at the University of South Florida.

Tamara Sonn, professor of Islamic studies at the University of South Florida, is author of *Between Qur'an and Crown: The Challenge of Political Legitimacy in the Arab World* (Westview, 1990), and *Interpreting Islam: Bandali Jawzi's Islamic Intellectual History* (Oxford, 1996). She is a member of the editorial boards of the *Middle East Studies Association Bulletin* and the *American Journal of Islamic Social Sciences*, and has contributed chapters and articles to numerous publications, including the *Oxford Encyclopedia of the Modern Islamic World*.

John O. Voll is professor of history at Georgetown University and Deputy Director of the Center for Muslim-Christian Understanding. Among his numerous publications are *Islam: Continuity and Change in the Modern World* (Syracuse, 1994, second edition), *Eighteenth-Century Renewal and Reform in Islam* (Syracuse, 1987) with N. Levtzion, and *The Contemporary Islamic Revival: A Critical Survey and Bibliography* (Greenwood, 1991) with Yvonne Y. Haddad and John L. Esposito.

South Florida Studies in the History of Judaism

240001	Lectures on Judaism in the Academy and in the Humanities	Neusner
240002	Lectures on Judaism in the History of Religion	Neusner
240003	Self-Fulfilling Prophecy: Exile and Return in the History of Judaism	Neusner
240004	The Canonical History of Ideas: The Place of the So-called Tannaite Midrashim, Mekhilta Attributed to R. Ishmael, Sifra, Sifré to Numbers, and Sifré to Deuteronomy	Neusner
240005	Ancient Judaism: Debates and Disputes, Second Series	Neusner
240006	The Hasmoneans and Their Supporters: From Mattathias to the Death of John Hyrcanus I	Sievers
240007	Approaches to Ancient Judaism: New Series, Volume One	Neusner
240008	Judaism in the Matrix of Christianity	Neusner
240009	Tradition as Selectivity: Scripture, Mishnah, Tosefta, and Midrash in the Talmud of Babylonia	Neusner
240010	The Tosefta: Translated from the Hebrew: Sixth Division Tohorot	Neusner
240011	In the Margins of the Midrash: Sifre Ha'azinu Texts, Commentaries and Reflections	Basser
240012	Language as Taxonomy: The Rules for Using Hebrew and Aramaic in the Babylonia Talmud	Neusner
240013	The Rules of Composition of the Talmud of Babylonia: The Cogency of the Bavli's Composite	Neusner
240014	Understanding the Rabbinic Mind: Essays on the Hermeneutic of Max Kadushin	Ochs
240015	Essays in Jewish Historiography	Rapoport-Albert
240016	The Golden Calf and the Origins of the Jewish Controversy	Bori/Ward
240017	Approaches to Ancient Judaism: New Series, Volume Two	Neusner
240018	The Bavli That Might Have Been: The Tosefta's Theory of Mishnah Commentary Compared With the Bavli's	Neusner
240019	The Formation of Judaism: In Retrospect and Prospect	Neusner
240020	Judaism in Society: The Evidence of the Yerushalmi,Toward the Natural History of a Religion	Neusner
240021	The Enchantments of Judaism: Rites of Transformation from Birth Through Death	Neusner
240022	Åbo Addresses	Neusner
240023	The City of God in Judaism and Other Comparative and Methodological Studies	Neusner
240024	The Bavli's One Voice: Types and Forms of Analytical Discourse and their Fixed Order of Appearance	Neusner
240025	The Dura-Europos Synagogue: A Re-evaluation (1932-1992)	Gutmann
240026	Precedent and Judicial Discretion: The Case of Joseph ibn Lev	Morell
240027	Max Weinreich Geschichte der jiddischen Sprachforschung	Frakes
240028	Israel: Its Life and Culture, Volume I	Pedersen
240029	Israel: Its Life and Culture, Volume II	Pedersen
240030	The Bavli's One Statement: The Metapropositional Program of Babylonian Talmud Tractate Zebahim Chapters One and Five	Neusner

South Florida Academic Commentary Series

243068	The Talmud of Babylonia, An Academic Commentary, Volume XXIII, Bavli Tractate Sanhedrin, B. Chapters VIII through XII	Neusner
243069	The Talmud of Babylonia, An Academic Commentary, Volume XIV, Bavli Tractate Ketubot, B. ChaptersVII through XIV	Neusner
243070	The Talmud of Babylonia, An Academic Commentary, Volume IV, Bavli Tractate Pesahim, B. Chapters VIII through XI	Neusner
243071	The Talmud of Babylonia, An Academic Commentary, Volume XXIX, Bavli Tractate Menahot, B. Chapters VII through XIV	Neusner
243072	The Talmud of Babylonia, An Academic Commentary, Volume XXVIII, Bavli Tractate Zebahim B. Chapters VIII through XV	Neusner
243073	The Talmud of Babylonia, An Academic Commentary, Volume XXI, Bavli Tractate Baba Mesia, B. Chapters VIII through XI	Neusner
243074	The Talmud of Babylonia, An Academic Commentary, Volume III, Bavli Tractate Erubin, A. ChaptersVI through XI	Neusner

South Florida-Rochester-Saint Louis
Studies on Religion and the Social Order

245001	Faith and Context, Volume 1	Ong
245002	Faith and Context, Volume 2	Ong
245003	Judaism and Civil Religion	Breslauer
245004	The Sociology of Andrew M. Greeley	Greeley
245005	Faith and Context, Volume 3	Ong
245006	The Christ of Michelangelo	Dixon
245007	From Hermeneutics to Ethical Consensus Among Cultures	Bori
245008	Mordecai Kaplan's Thought in a Postmodern Age	Breslauer
245009	No Longer Aliens, No Longer Strangers	Eckardt
245010	Between Tradition and Culture	Ellenson
245011	Religion and the Social Order	Neusner
245012	Christianity and the Stranger	Nichols
245013	The Polish Challenge	Czosnyka
245014	Islam and the Question of Minorities	Sonn

South Florida International Studies in
Formative Christianity and Judaism

242501	The Earliest Christian Mission to 'All Nations'	La Grand
242502	Judaic Approaches to the Gospels	Chilton
252403	The "Essence of Christianity"	Forni Rosa
242504	The Wicked Tenants and Gethsemane	Aus